Essential Italy

by Jane Shaw

Jane Shaw grew up in Edinburgh and lived in London for several years before fleeing to Rome in the early 1990s, where she lives in the heart of Trastevere, writing, editing and translating. She has contributed to a wide range of guide books, both to Rome and the whole of Italy and this is her second AA Essential guide, her first being *Essential Rome*.

Above: *reflections in the Grand Canal, Venice*

AA Publishing

Pigeons in Venice's St Mark's square settle on welcoming arms

Find out more about AA Publishing and the wide range of services the AA provides by visiting our website at www.theAA.com

Written by Jane Shaw

Published by AA Publishing, a trading name of Automobile Association Developments Limited, whose registered office is Millstream, Maidenhead Road, Wiondsor, berkshire, SL4 5GD.
Registered number 1878835.

Reprinted 2003. Information verified and updated.

A CIP catalogue record for this book is available from the British Library.

ISBN 0 7495 1915 0

A01088

Colour separation: Pace Colour, Southampton
Printed and bound in Italy by Printer Trento S.r.l.

Contents

About this Book

KEY TO SYMBOLS

- map reference to the maps found in the What to See section
- address or location
- telephone number
- opening times
- restaurant or café on premises or near by
- nearest underground train station
- nearest bus/tram route
- nearest overground train station
- ferry crossings and boat excursions
- travel by air
- tourist information
- facilities for visitors with disabilities
- admission charge
- other places of interest near by
- other practical information
- ➤ indicates the page where you will find a fuller description

Essential *Italy* is divided into five sections to cover the most important aspects of your visit to Italy.

Viewing Italy pages 5–14
An introduction to Italy by the author.
Italy's Features
Essence of Italy
The Shaping of Italy
Peace and Quiet
Italy's Famous

Top Ten pages 15–26
The author's choice of the Top Ten places to see in Italy, listed in alphabetical order, each with practical information.

What to See pages 27–90
The five main areas of Italy, each with its own brief introduction and an alphabetical listing of the main attractions.
Practical information
Snippets of 'Did you know...' information
2 suggested walks
4 suggested tours (including 2 boat trips)
2 features

Where To... pages 91–116
Detailed listings of the best places to eat, stay, shop, take the children and be entertained.

Practical Matters pages 117–24
A highly visual section containing essential travel information.

Maps
All map references are to the individual maps found in the What to See section of this guide.

For example, Palermo has the reference 29C1 – indicating the page on which the map is located and the grid square in which the city is to be found. A list of the maps that have been used in this travel guide can be found in the index.

Prices
Where appropriate, an indication of the cost of an establishment is given by € signs:

€€€ denotes higher prices, €€ denotes average prices, while € denotes lower charges.

Star Ratings
Most of the places described in this book have been given a separate rating:

✪✪✪	Do not miss
✪✪	Highly recommended
✪	Worth seeing

Viewing Italy

Above: *a balcony garden defies peeling stucco*
Right: *Italy's Mediterranean climate invites sun-worship*

Jane Shaw's Italy

Read All About It
Whole books have been dedicated to an appreciation of Italy, although not all of them are full of gushing praise; Charles Dickens, for example, had some pretty damning things to say about some of the sights he describes in *Pictures from Italy*. Other writers on Italy include Goethe (*An Italian Journey*), Henry James (*Italian Hours*) and D H Lawrence (*D H Lawrence and Italy*). For an up-to-date account of an Englishman's life in Italy, try Tim Parks' ever-expanding list of works.

It's difficult to say anything original about Italy, although one of the most rewarding things about living here is the realisation that there is far more to the country than what is expressed in the rather romanticised or jaundiced views of its many home-grown and foreign admirers and critics. Yes, it's full of stunning towns and cities full of unbelievably beautiful buildings and populated by attractive, friendly people whose musical language makes the most banal of observations sound poetic (until you understand them), but the life that is going on is just as real as it is in any other European country. Sure, things don't always work the way you would like them to, and you may spend half a day paying a cheque into your bank account or queuing up in some state office to collect yet more of the seemingly interminable list of documents you need to prove who you are and where you live. But a lot of this is improving, and the more forgiving attitude that prevails means people are less likely to jump down your throat when it is you who have made the mistake.

Even if you are only here for a few days, you are likely to have several surprises – some good and some bad. Be flexible, relax and you can't go wrong; the museum you have gone out of your way to see may be shut when it should be open, but instead you might end up having a memorable lunch in an ordinary-looking restaurant where, after the coffee, the proprietor plies you with some ambrosian *digestivo* made from the fruit in his own orchard.

San Gimignano, famed for its medieval towers, is always popular with tourists

Italy's Features

The Country

Italy covers a famously boot-shaped area of slightly over 300,000sq km, stretching for 1,300km from the Alps in the north to Sicily, level with the northern tip of Africa, in the south. About 25 per cent of this area is covered by plains (such as that of the River Po) and the rest is hilly or mountainous. There are 7,500km of coastline.

The People

Just over 50 per cent of the nearly 58 million people living in Italy today live in towns of at least 20,000 inhabitants. Until Unification in 1870, the Italian nation did not exist; the country was divided into several small states, each with its own history and culture. Regionalism is still strong throughout Italy and not just at the level of cuisine and dialect; each of the 20 regions has a degree of political autonomy.

Worker Movements

One of the side affects of Italy's economic boom has been the reversal of emigration habits. Until 1974 Italy exported workers; since then (and particularly since the late 1980s), the outward flow has turned into an influx of immigrants, particularly from northern Africa, eastern Europe, the Philippines and the USA, and now there are more than 1.2 million foreigners registered as resident in Italy.

Below: *Chianti vineyards are the source of Italy's best-known wine*
Inset: *shoppers in Milan*

Economy

Since World War II Italy has found itself among the top ten world economic powers, although nearly all of this wealth is in the north. Its main agricultural crops include olives, grapes, wheat, rice and tomatoes and among its main industries are fashion, motor vehicles, domestic appliances, pasta and tourism.

Essence of Italy

Italy has one of the oldest tourist industries in the world, having been among the principal meccas for rich northern European and American 'grand tourists' in the 18th and 19th centuries. They came here to sample the ancient, Renaissance and baroque delights of Venice, Florence and Tuscany, Rome, Naples and (for the more adventurous) Sicily. These places still have an enormous pull, attracting millions of visitors every year. But unless you are really short of time, don't limit yourself to mainstream tourist Italy. Almost anywhere is within reach of little towns and villages, isolated ancient remains, mountains or the sea, so make the most of these delights for a richly varied stay in one of the world's most beautiful countries.

Below: *the instantly recognisable Venetian waterfront*
Inset: *Canova's sensuous statue of Pauline Borghese in Rome's Borghese Gallery*

THE 10 ESSENTIALS

If you only have a short time to visit Italy, or would like to get a really complete picture of the country, here are the essentials:

- **Enjoy the art**: select a few artists and notice the variety and geographical spread of the works that each has left (➤ 14 and ➤ 27–90).
- **Spend at least half a day** without a map or guide book in the historic centre of a city or large town, and just soak up the atmosphere.
- **Spend an afternoon over lunch** in typical Italian style and slip into a more relaxed pace of life (➤ 38–39 and ➤ 92–99).
- **Visit at least one ancient site**, even if it's just a Roman amphitheatre. There is bound to be one within reach of where you are staying.
- **Spend a day on the beach**; hire an umbrella and sun-bed and watch the world go by.
- **Visit at least one of the smaller towns**: many contain architectural treasures to compare with those of the great cities, and have a timeless ambience all their own (➤ 27–90).
- **Eat ice-creams** wherever you go and compare them. The variety of flavours will astonish you.
- **See some mountains or lakes** and enjoy a bit of the outdoor life (➤ 12–13, 34–35, 47, 81).
- **Attend an outdoor play**, opera or concert – an enchanting experience in Italy's generally benign climate (➤ 110–12).
- **Take a trip to an island**: some, like Capri, are beautiful tourist honeypots, while others offer peace and quiet off the beaten track (➤ 12–13, ➤ 34, 61, 86).

Above: *sun, sea and sand are in plentiful supply...*
Below: *...as are delicious ice-creams of infinite variety*

The Shaping of Italy

Julius Caesar was ruler of the Roman world in the 1st century BC but he never became emperor

9th century BC
First settlements in Etruria (North Central).

753 BC
Founding of Rome.

509 BC
Roman Republic established.

312 BC
Via Appia built.

27 BC
Augustus becomes first Roman Emperor.

AD 79
Pompei buried during the eruption of Vesuvius.

117
Roman Empire at its zenith.

324
Christianity becomes the Imperial state religion.

395
Empire divided into two sections, Eastern and Western; Ravenna is seat of Western Empire (from *c*402).

475
Fall of Western Empire to barbarians.

535–53
Eastern Emperor recaptures Western Empire.

564
Lombards conquer Italy from the north.

609
Pantheon in Rome consecrated as a church.

800
Charlemagne crowned Emperor in St Peter's, Rome.

962
Holy Roman Empire founded by Otto I.

11th century
Norman conquests of Sicily and southern Italy.

1076
First quarrels between supporters of the Pope (Guelphs) and of the Emperor (Ghibellines).

1094
New San Marco in Venice is consecrated.

1167
Lombard League founded to counter the Emperor.

1250
Papacy triumphs over Holy Roman Empire.

1302
Anjou dynasty established in Naples.

1305–77
'Babylonian' period for Papacy as it moves to Avignon under pressure from French.

1321
Publication of Dante's *Divine Comedy*.

1378–1415
Great Schism between Pope in Rome and Antipopes in Pisa and Avignon.

1442
Alfonso of Aragon captures and becomes king of the Two Sicilies.

1541
Michelangelo finishes the Sistine Chapel frescoes.

1559
Treaty of Cateau-Cambrèsis establishes Spanish domination of Naples, Sicily, Sardinia and Milan.

1748
Excavation of Pompei begins.

1796
Napoleon's campaign in Lombardy.

1797
Treaty of Campo Formio gives Venice to Austria, while France controls the rest of northern Italy.

1805
Napoleon crowned king of the Lombards.

1808–9
Rome occupied by the French. Papal States annexed; Pope taken to France as prisoner.

1814
Defeat of Napoleon; Pope back in Rome.

1815
Congress of Vienna; Austria keeps Venice.

1831
Mazzini founds *Giovane Italia* movement; start of Risorgimento.

1848
Year of revolutions.

1849
Brief 'Republic of Rome' defeated by French.

1859
Piedmont gets Lombardy, Parma, Modena and Tuscany from Austria.

1860
Garibaldi and the Thousand capture the Kingdom of the Two Sicilies.

1861
Kingdom of Italy proclaimed with capital in Turin and Vittorio Emanuele II as King.

1866
Italy wins Venice back from Austria.

1870
Italy united, with Rome as its capital.

1922
Fascist march on Rome; Mussolini forms government.

1935
Italy invades Ethiopia. Ethiopia annexed following year.

1939
Italy annexes Albania, across the Adriatic.

1940
Italy joins Axis and enters World War II.

Crowds applaud liberating US troops as they enter Milan on 1 April, 1945

Benito Mussolini in dictatorial stance

1943
Allies land in Sicily. Mussolini arrested as Italy surrenders. He's later rescued by the Nazis.

1945
Liberation of Italy from the Nazis. Mussolini is arrested again and shot.

1946
First Republic is founded.

1957
Treaty of Rome founds European Union.

1960
Film director Frederico Fellini encapsualtes the era in *La Dolce Vita*.

1992
Exposure of widespread political corruption and collapse of Christian Democrat Party, powerful in post-war period.

2002
Along with most of the EU, Italy adopts the single currency (Euro).

Peace & Quiet

Although the country's art and history are the attractions for most visitors to Italy, there are also plenty of places to view nature at its best. The Italian tradition of spending August in the mountains or by the sea means that many of these areas are very busy in the height of summer, yet it is always possible to find tranquil spots in which to unwind.

National Parks

National parks, with their mapped and way-marked walking trails, are the best places to explore Italy's mountain ranges. Parco Nazionale del Gran Paradiso in the northwest is the most famous. In summer, walkers can enjoy its spectacular Alpine scenery and plant life and look out for the ibex, a rare member of the deer family with thick, ridged horns. Parco Nazionale dello Stelvio, on the edges of the Dolomiti (Dolomites) (➤ 47), is home to ibex, chamois and eagles. To its south is the Parco Nazionale delle Incisioni Rupestri, with neolithic rock carvings. Parco Nazionale dei Monti Sibillini is set in the ruggedly pretty northern Apennines, while the Parco dell'Orecchiella is a good base for exploring the Alpi Apuane of Tuscany. Smaller areas of natural beauty are often protected as nature reserves (*parco naturale* or *riserva*). These are found all over Italy and usually have marked walking routes as well as other facilities such as picnic areas and visitors' information centres. For more details try www.ctsviaggi.com/parchionline

Top: *fine walking country in Abruzzo, south central Italy*
Inset: *the spectacular horned ibex*

Islands

The coast of Italy is surrounded by groups of pretty little islands. Although some islands become extremely crowded in summer, many remain off the beaten track and most archipelagos have at least one island that remains relatively peaceful, especially if you avoid mid-July to the end of August. Thus fashionable Ponza off the Lazio coast lies close to unspoilt Ventotenne (both accessible from Formia), while serene Procida is next to throbbing Capri

(➤ 86) and Ischia (all reached via Naples). North of Gargano (➤ 87) are the rugged Isole Tremiti (reached from Vieste). Sicily has three particularly attractive island clusters: the Isole Eolie (via Naples and Palermo) which include the busy Lipari and the more peaceful Stromboli; the Isole Egadi (via Palermo and Trapani) whose main island is Favignana, while Marettimo and Levanzo are less populated; and the Isole Pelagie (via Agrigento), which nestle above Tunisia. Also off Sicily are the isolated islands of Ustica (via Naples and Palermo) in the north, and Pantelleria (via Trapani and Agrigento) to the southwest.

Lakes

For those who like to combine mountain scenery with watersports, lakes are the answer. Prime among these are the Great Lakes of the north – Como (➤ 35), Garda, Iseo, Maggiore (➤ 34), Orta and Varese; but there are also several major lakes in central Italy. Within easy striking distance of Rome are the lakes of Bracciano, Vico (both northwest) and Nemi (southeast), all of which become busy weekend playgrounds during the summer. North of Viterbo is Lago di Bolsena, and the atmospheric Lago Trasimeno lies on the Umbrian-Tuscan border.

Top: *placid now, Lago di Bolsena occupies a huge volcanic crater*
Inset: *a Sicilian olive grove – an age-old scene*

Italy's Famous

Italian Explorers
Christopher Columbus was not the only Italian to extend the frontiers of the known world. Two centuries earlier, the Venetian Marco Polo (1254–1324) made his historic overland trek to China, where he stayed for about 20 years before returning home to write his (slightly exaggerated) *Book of Marvels*. Giovanni Caboto (John Cabot), who sailed from Bristol, England, to discover Canada in 1497, was born in Gaeta, north of Naples, while the newly found continent of America was named after Italian Amerigo Vespucci in 1507, when he was (inaccurately) credited with discovering it.

Two great masters of 19th-century Italian opera: Puccini (right) and Verdi (below)

In Art and Music

European painting, sculpture, architecture and classical music (especially opera) owe a huge debt to generations of Italian geniuses. Italy's host of great artists includes: Giotto di Bondone (1267–1337), a forefather of the Renaissance whose exquisite frescoes can be seen all over central and northeastern Italy; Filippo Brunelleschi (1377–1446), the revolutionary architect and sculptor most celebrated as creator of the magnificent dome of Florence's cathedral; Masaccio (1401–28) who, during a tragically short life, left paintings that were to act as lessons in style for subsequent generations; the exquisite painter Piero della Francesca (1415–92), much admired in our modern age; and the big three – Leonardo da Vinci (1452–1519), Michelangelo Buonarroti (1475–1564) and Raphael (1483–1520). The vigorous, flamboyant works of Titian (1485–1576) and Tintoretto (1518–94), and the dramatic canvases of Caravaggio (1571–1610), were also influential in the history of painting.

The Italian contribution to music includes Claudio Monteverdi (1567–1643), the 'inventor' of opera, as well as Gioaichino Rossini (1792–1868), Giuseppe Verdi (1813–1901) and Giacomo Puccini (1858–1924), who all helped to establish Italy as the capital of lyrical opera.

In Science and Technology

Italians have also made major discoveries in the world of science and technology. In the 17th century Galileo Galilei invented the telescope and discovered that the earth revolved around the sun, rather than vice versa. This discovery was to cost him his freedom, when a less than technology-friendly church condemned him for heresy. Forced to recant, he spent his last years under house arrest. Later, in 1801, Alessandro Volta's first battery was to prove less controversial, while Guglielmo Marconi's invention of the radio was enthusiastically received by the science-minded society of the late 19th century.

Top Ten

Above: *a touch of charm in the grand interior of St Peter's Basilica, Rome*
Right: *elegantly uniformed tourist police in Milan*

1
Basilica San Pietro & Il Vaticano (St Peter's & the Vatican)

72A3

Vatican Tourist Office
06 6968 662

Ottaviano

To Piazza del Risorgimento

Basilica San Pietro

Apr–Sep, 7–7; Oct–Mar, 7–6

Basilica: free; roof: moderate

Musei Vaticani

06 6988 3041

Mar–Nov, Mon–Sat 8:45–2:20; Dec–Feb, Mon–Sat 8:45–12:20; last Sun of month 8:45–12:20

Cafeteria (€)

Good

Expensive; free last Sun of month

St Peter's Square

One of the world's biggest churches half fills one of its smallest states – the Vatican, headquarters of the Roman Catholic church and home to a vast museum.

The first St Peter's was built by Emperor Constantine over the saint's tomb, which is in the crypt. Today's awesome building was started in 1503, when Pope Julius II appointed Bramante as architect. Work lasted for more than 120 years and many important architects and artists were involved. Bramante's floor plan is 187m long (the lengths of other cathedrals are marked on the central nave); Michelangelo designed the 132.5m-high dome, Carlo Maderno the façade, and Bernini the impressive oval colonnade outside the basilica.

Inside, on the right, is Michelangelo's *Pietà* of 1499. Other gems include a 13th-century bronze statue of St Peter, its foot worn away by the touch of pilgrims; Bernini's huge *Baldacchino* (under which only the pope can celebrate mass), and his monuments to popes Urban VIII and Alexander VII; and Giotto's mosaic of an angel.

The spectacular view from the roof is framed by massive statues of Christ, John the Baptist and the Apostles (minus St Peter).

Behind the basilica lie the vast **Vatican museums.** There is far too much for one visit, but you can select one of several recommended timed routes to see a selection of the highlights. These include: the Museo Gregoriano-

Egizio Egyptian collection; the Museo Chiaramonti collection of Roman sculpture; the Museo Pio Clementine, whose ancient art includes the *Belvedere Apollo* and *Laocoön*; the Museo Gregoriano–Etrusco's Greek, Roman and Etruscan art; and corridors of tapestries and 16th-century maps of the Italian regions leading to one of the main attractions, the four Raphael rooms. These were painted between 1508 and 1525 (the last was finished after Raphael's death in 1520). In the first room is the famous *School of Athens* in which many of Raphael's contemporaries are portrayed as Greek philosophers and poets. The other rooms show biblical and early Christian scenes, significant events in papal history, and the story of Constantine.

Next comes the legendary **Sistine Chapel**. Michelangelo painted the ceiling between 1508 and 1512, crouching for hours on scaffolding as Pope Julius II chivvied him on from below. A thorough (and controversial) cleaning in the 1980s and 1990s, during which some of the garments that more prudish popes had had painted on to Michelangelo's scantily clad biblical figures were stripped off, along with the dust and grime, has restored its original vibrant colours. The ceiling tells the story of the Creation, in which a pink-clad God is busy dividing light from darkness and water from land before creating the sun, the moon, Adam and Eve. The last four panels show the birth of original sin and the story of Noah. On the chapel's end wall is Michelangelo's much later *Last Judgement*. While he painted this (1534–41) he was racked with ill-health and thoughts of mortality, and the flayed skin held up by St Bartholomew (to Christ's left) is believed to be a self-portrait. The other walls were painted by, among others, Botticelli, Ghirlandaio and Perugino.

Top: *Michelangelo's extraordinary Sistine Chapel ceiling*
Inset: *visitors dwarfed by mighty columns in St Peter's Basilica*

Beyond the chapel are: the Vatican library with over 1 million valuable volumes; a gallery of modern religious art, including works by Klee, Munch and Picasso; and collections of pagan and early Christian antiquities. The Pinacoteca (picture gallery) has a marvellous collection of medieval, Renaissance and baroque paintings with masterpieces by most of the famous names in European art, including Caravaggio, Raphael and Leonardo da Vinci.

2
Costiera Amalfitana (Amalfi Coast)

 29C2

Ravello

Piazza Duomo 10
089 857 096;
www.ravelloapts.org

Pompei (➤ 24)

Amalfi

Corso delle Repubbliche Marinare 27–29
089 871 107

South of Naples lies a 30km stretch of spectacular coastline, where ragged, grey cliffs plunge into an unbelievably turquoise Mediterranean.

Although natural beauty, picturesque architecture, a good climate and excellent local cuisine have combined to make this one of Italy's busiest holiday haunts, it is still possible, among the summer crowds that fill the white fishing-villages-turned-resorts, to feel the romance that has inspired generations of artists and songwriters.

Even the slightly overdeveloped Sorrento, a centre for package tours on the western end of the Costiera, has its peaceful, flower-filled corners, with views over the twinkling Bay of Naples to the islands of Capri (➤ 86) and Ischia. Further east is the more chic and expensive resort of Positano, clinging to the cliffside, with some of the best beaches in the area.

North and a little inland from here is **Ravello**, arguably the most stunning of the Amalfitana towns. The sea views are particularly good from exotic Villa Rufolo, which has parts that date back to the 11th century. Wagner stayed here in 1880 and based the magic gardens in *Parsifal* on those of the villa. The gardens of the Villa Cimbrone are equally evocative. Ravello's 11th-century Cathedral of San Pantaleone was renovated in the 18th century, but the bronze doors by Barisano da Trani (1179) have survived along with other elements of the earlier building, including an ornate 13th-century pulpit.

Amalfi is the Costiera's largest town and, until the 12th century, it was a major maritime power. Its most eye-catching sight is the 9th-century Cathedral of Sant'Andrea – although the sumptuous façade is a 19th-century restoration of a 13th-century original. Alongside is the 13th-century Chiostro del Paradiso (Cloister of Paradise) where Amalfi's most illustrious citizens were laid to rest.

Romantic Sorrento makes a convenient base for exploring the Amalfi Coast

3

Duomo di Milano (Milan Cathedral)

This massive yet delicate Gothic building towering above its own vast, open piazza, is dramatically surrounded by bustling, modern Milan.

Even allowing for the decades it usually took to complete a cathedral, the Duomo of Milan was a long time in the making. Work started in 1386 under Prince Gian Galeazzo Visconti, continued over the following centuries in the hands of a host of European craftsmen, and was finished in 1809 under the orders of Napoleon. A trip on to the roof, with its views over Milan to the Alps glimpsed through a forest of 135 icing-sugar spires and 2,244 statues, makes the long centuries of toil seem worthwhile.

28A4

02 7202 2656

Cafeteria (€)

Museo: 9:30–12:30, 3–6; roof: 9–5; treasury and crypt: 9–12, 2:30–6; baptistery: 9:45–5:45

Few

Museo and roof: moderate; treasury and crypt: cheap

At 157m long and 92m wide, this is the third-largest church in Europe after St Peter's (➤ 16) and Seville Cathedral. The façade is a surprisingly harmonious mishmash of styles from Gothic, through Renaissance and baroque to neo-classical. Beyond the bas-relief bronze doors depicting scenes from the lives of the Virgin and St Ambrose (Milan's patron saint), as well as Milanese history, is a contrastingly bare interior with 52 columns, each 148m high, and numerous tombs and memorials lit by glorious 15th- and 16th-century stained-glass windows. Look out in particular for a 12th-century bronze candelabrum and the gruesome statue of the flayed St Bartholomew holding his skin. The repeated symbol of a snake swallowing a man was the local Visconti family crest. The crypt contains the usual church treasures as well as traces of the original 4th-century baptistery.

In the Museo del Duomo (Cathedral Museum), to the south, the history of the cathedral's construction is illustrated alongside historic artefacts.

The filigree façade of Milan Cathedral, described by Mark Twain as a 'poem in marble'

4

Foro Romano, Palatino & Colosseo (Roman Forum, Palatine Hill & Colosseum)

These atmospheric ruins, behind the headquarters of today's city council, represent the social, political, religious and business heart of ancient Rome.

The Colosseum – a lasting monument to Roman bloodlust

Foro and Palatino

 72C3, 72C2

 Via dei Fori Imperiali

 06 3996 7700

Apr–Sep, daily 9–7:30; Oct–Mar, 9–5 (last admission 3). Closed 1 Jan and 25 Dec

Few

Foro free; Palatino expensive (includes Colosseo)

Colosseo

73D2

Piazza del Colosseo

06 3996 7700

Apr–Sep, 9–7:30; Oct–Mar, 9–5:30

Very few

Included in Palatino

You are immersed in Rome's history as soon as you enter the Forum. Left of the entrance is the Basilica Aemilia with traces of coins fused into its floor from a fire in the 5th century. Next, along the Sacred Way, is the (rebuilt) 3rd-century Curia where the Senate met, and the rostrum where orations were made. Opposite the Curia are three beautiful columns from the Temple of Castor and Pollux. The round building is the Temple of Vesta – the vestal virgins lived in the villa behind it. Opposite are the three massive vaults of the 4th-century AD Basilica of Maxentius and Constantine (much studied by Renaissance architects). The Arch of Titus, near the exit, was erected in the 1st century AD to celebrate the Emperor's sack of Jerusalem.

On the Palatine Hill overlooking the Forum are the remains of the emperors' gigantic palaces and traces of 7th-century BC huts, possibly from Romulus' time.

The Colosseum was built by Emperor Vespasian in the 1st century AD. Tiered seating for more than 55,000 blood-thirsty spectators overlooked a central ring where gladiators, mismatched combatants and wild animals (kept in underground passages) fought each other to the death. Mock sea battles could also be staged, thanks to an underground water supply which allowed the arena to be flooded if required. Changing public taste forced the Colosseum into disuse in the mid-6th century.

5

Galleria degli Uffizi, Firenze (Uffizi Gallery, Florence)

Generations of the powerful Medici family amassed this collection of 13th- to 18th-century paintings, which is among the finest in the world.

Giorgio Vasari designed the building in 1560 to house the Medici's art collections and administrative offices (*uffici*). The art was bequeathed to the city of Florence in 1737 by Anna Maria Luisa, the last of the Medici dynasty. Inside, 45 galleries bristle with world-famous masterpieces hung in roughly chronological order to give an opulent overview of the development of mainly Italian art.

Early highlights include Giotto's *Ognissanti Madonna* (1310), showing his – for its time – revolutionary naturalism and use of perspective. Contrast it with the flatter Gothic styles of Simone Martini, Cimabue and Duccio. Throughout the 15th century the representation of perspective developed as the Renaissance got under way. Look for this in Paolo Uccello's *Battle of San Romano* (1456), Piero della Francesca's imposing profiles of the Duke and Duchess of Urbino (1465–70) and Fra Filippo Lippi's *Virgin and Child*. The magnificent Botticelli collection includes the *Birth of Venus* (1485) and *Primavera* (1478) and there are two Leonardo da Vinci works: an *Annunciation* (1472–5) and an unfinished *Adoration of the Magi* (1481).

Michelangelo's *Holy Family* (1456), with its contorted poses and sculpted, draped fabrics, is an early example of Mannerism, which evolved throughout the following century. Highlights from this period include Raphael's *Madonna of the Goldfinch* (1506), Parmigianino's *Madonna of the Long Neck* (1534), Titian's sultry *Venus of Urbino* (1538) and works by Caravaggio. Among the non-Italian masters represented at the Uffizi are Cranach, Dürer, Holbein, Rubens, Van Dyck, Goya and Rembrandt.

59D4

Loggiata degli Uffizi 6

055 238 8651

Tue–Fri, Sun 8:30–7, Sat 8:30–10 (booking advised). Closed Mon, 1 Jan, 1 May, 25 Dec

Cafeteria (€)

3, 11, 15, 23

Good

Expensive

Other Florence sights (➤ 53–6)

Uffizi's extensive collection of sculpture

6
Lecce

29D2

Corso Vittorio Emanuele 24 0832 248 092

Salentino (➤ 88)

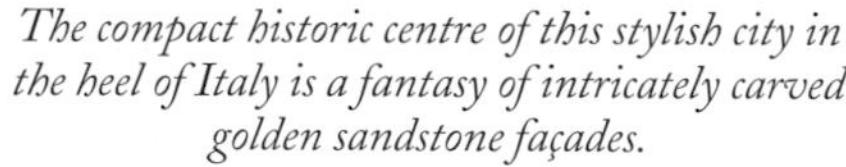

The compact historic centre of this stylish city in the heel of Italy is a fantasy of intricately carved golden sandstone façades.

In imperial Roman times Lecce, then called Lupiae, was an important centre. There are two well-preserved relics from this period: a 1st-century BC amphitheatre in Piazza Sant'Oronzo and a Roman theatre off Via Paladini. The column in the piazza is also Roman and originally stood at the end of the Via Appia in Brindisi (➤ 85). An 18th-century bronze of St Oronzo (the town's patron) graces its top.

Baroque Lecce owes its existence to a period of prosperity in the 15th to 17th centuries when the city was a strategic centre for Europe's continuous struggles against the Ottoman Empire. Using the soft local stone, architects were able to create voluptuous masses of exquisitely carved fruit, flowers, *putti* and saints to adorn palaces and churches. These delicate details make for a far lighter style of building than that of the more monumental baroque in other cities. Among the best examples of baroque Lecce is Santa Croce (1549–1679). Gabriele Riccardi started the façade and Giuseppe Zimbalo (called lo Zingarello) added the decoration in the 17th century; he was also responsible for the next-door Palazzo del Governo (Governor's Palace). Another lo Zingarello gem is the Duomo (1659–70), with its Egyptian-influenced 68m-high campanile. The Palazzo Vescovile and Seminario (Bishop's Palace and Seminary, 1709) are by lo Zingarello's pupil, Giuseppe Cino. Also worth a visit are: lo Zingarello's Rosario, his last work, dating from 1691; the Norman church of Santi Nicolò e Cataldo, which was extensively added to in 1716; and the Museo Provinciale Sigismondo Castromediano (Provincial Museum), which has an excellent collection of ceramics.

The exuberant baroque façade of the Basilica of Santa Croce in Lecce

7

Piazza San Marco, Venezia (St Mark's Square, Venice)

Generations of Venetians and visitors have frequented the smart, porticoed cafés that flank this vast, paved square.

28B4

Plenty of cafés (€€€)

Basilica San Marco

041 522 5205

Mon–Sat 10–5, Sun 2–5. Closed during services

Moderate

Museo Correr

041 522 5625

Apr–Oct, 9–7; Nov–Mar, 9–5 (Nov–Apr closes 4)

Expensive

The northwest side of the square is dominated by the squat, ornate façade of **Basilica San Marco**, built between 1063 and 1073 to replace an older building. Above the main entrance are copies of four 2nd-century BC bronze horses, brought to Venice in 1204. Above the arches are some exquisite 13th-century carvings and further up are mosaics of the life of St Mark. Virtually every surface of the opulent interior, including the floor, is decorated with mosaics (mostly 12th to 14th centuries). Gold-rich treasures, such as the 10th-century *Pala d'Oro* altarpiece and the *Madonna di Nicopeia* (1204), reflect Venice's strong Byzantine links. The treasury and Museo Marciano house more priceless artefacts (including the original bronze horses). There are wonderful views from the 100m-high campanile.

Next to the basilica is the Palazzo Reale (Royal Palace), residence of the Doges of Venice since the 9th century; the present Gothic building is late 14th century. Inside are the theatrically imposing meeting rooms of the élite groups who ran Venice's complex internal and foreign affairs. These are lined with dark wood and massive wall and ceiling paintings, many by Tintoretto and Veronese. The presence of a torture chamber and a labyrinth of dank prison cells hints at the far from benign nature of some aspects of Venetian government. Unfortunate suspects were brought into the prison via the famous Bridge of Sighs behind the *palazzo*.

The **Museo Correr** is at the opposite end of the piazza. It has a fine collection of paintings from the Renaissance onwards.

Elegant St Mark's Square

8
Pompei

29C2

Piazza Esedra 5, Pompei

081 536 5154; www.pompeiisites.org

Apr–Oct, 8:30–7:30; Nov–Mar, 8:30–5 (last admission 3:30). Closed 1 Jan and 25 Dec

Cafeteria (€)

Good

Expensive

Costiera Amalfitana (➤ 18)

Vesuvius broods over the ruins of the city it destroyed in AD 79

The remains of this busy ancient city, buried when Vesuvius erupted in AD 79, give some poignant glimpses of daily life in the Roman empire.

Pompei has been under excavation for more than 250 years and, although only a few buildings are open to the public, there is far too much to see in one day. It is best to buy a detailed guide and map, visit your priority sights, and then wander to absorb the unique atmosphere of this beautiful site. Many of the major artistic finds are on show in the Museo Archeologico Nazionale (National Archaeological Museum) in Naples (➤ 84).

Among the most interesting houses are patrician and middle-class villas with statues, mosaics and frescoes, many of them erotic and/or mystic and difficult to interpret. Try to see the Casa dei Vetii, the Casa del Fauno, the Casa del Poeta Tragico with its 'beware of the dog' sign and, if it's open, the Casa dei Misteri. Shops include a bakery, a cramped brothel with graphic wall paintings of the services offered, and a laundry where you can follow the complicated washing procedures used by ancient Romans. There are also numerous bars and food shops, many with large clay storage pots embedded into their serving hatches.

Public buildings include the forum with its basilica and temples, two theatres, Italy's oldest surviving amphitheatre (80 BC), baths and two gyms.

Throughout Pompei the cobbled streets are heavily grooved by the passage of inumerable carts, and the walls are spattered with snatches of carefully executed graffiti. The most moving memorials of the disaster are the casts of bodies of the victims (believed to be about 10 per cent of the 25,000 population), eternally frozen in the positions in which they died.

9
Ravenna's Mosaics

Ravenna's delightful early Christian mosaics are some of the best in Europe, with their unusual mix of classical and Byzantine influences.

While much of the rest of western Europe was in Dark Ages decline, Ravenna was enjoying a period of prosperity as an important provincial centre and, from around AD 402, as the western capital of the Roman Empire. The city had converted to Christianity in the 2nd century and much of its wealth went into building and decorating churches and other religious sites. The mosaics contain some of the earliest versions of now well-known Christian images such as the baptism of Christ, the Virgin, saints, martyrs and apostles with their symbols, and the cross. The best are housed in five sites across the historic centre.

The 5th-century **Battistero (Baptistery) Neoniano** is believed to be Ravenna's oldest monument. The mosaics show the baptism of Christ and the 12 apostles. The cruciform **Mausoleo (Mausoleum) di Galla Placidia** (started 430) may not contain the remains of the strong-willed Galla, but it does have charming mosaics of stars and flowers on the vaults and a Good Shepherd on the west wall. The dome of the **Battistero degli Ariani** (late 5th century) shows another baptism of Christ.

The finest mosaics in Ravenna are in two churches. **Sant'Apollinare Nuovo** (AD 519) contains processions of saints bearing gifts to the Virgin and scenes from the life of Christ, all with gold backgrounds. **San Vitale** (consecrated AD 547) has richly coloured mosaics full of flowers and birds and depicting Christ the King, Old Testament scenes, and Empress Theodora and Emperor Justinian.

28B4

Summer 9–7; winter 9–4:30. Closed 1 Jan and 25 Dec

Via Salara 8/12
0544 35404;
www.comune.ravenna.it/turismo/

Take advantage of one of the multi-entrance ticket options

Battistero Neoniano

Via Battistero

Mausoleo di Galla Placidia

Via Fiandrini

Battistero degli Ariani

Via degli Ariani

Sant'Apollinare Nuovo

Via di Roma

San Vitale

Via Fiandrini

Mosaics line the little mausoleum of Roman matron Galla Placidia

10

Valle dei Templi, Sicilia (Valley of the Temples, Sicily)

Noble remains in the ancient Greek temple complex at Agrigento

The most extensive ancient Greek remains outside Greece, these nine ruined 6th- and 5th-century BC *temples were once part of the city of Akragas.*

29C1

Via dei Templi, Agrigento; Via Sacra, Agrigento

0922 20454

8:30 to one hour before sunset

Restaurant (€€€)

Bus from Agrigento

Tourist office in Agrigento 0922 20454

Akragas (now Agrigento) was founded in 582 BC by settlers from Rhodes. For nearly 200 years it flourished, boasting a temple complex that rivalled that of Athens. In 406 BC, Akragas was attacked by the Carthaginians, who pillaged the temples. Destruction was continued by zealous 6th-century Christians and earthquakes.

Eight of the temples lie west to east along a ridge south of Agrigento and can be visited in a day on foot. Very little remains of the Tempio di Vulcano (430 BC) but near by is a group of shrines for sacrifices to the underground (chthonic) gods. The strikingly positioned three columns are part of the so-called Tempio dei Dioscuri (Castor and Pollux), a 19th-century assemblage of bits and pieces from several buildings. Further on is the unfinished Tempio di Giove (Olympian Zeus), started in 480 BC. At 113m by 56m, it would have been the biggest Doric temple ever built. Eight erect columns belong to the Tempio di Ercole (Hercules), built in 520 BC and probably the oldest survivor in the valley. The Tempio della Concordia (Concord, 430 BC) is uniquely well preserved, having been used as a church in the 6th century. The 450 BC Tempio di Hera (Juno) is set dramatically on top of the ridge. A few hundred metres south is the Tempio di Esculapio (Aesculepius, god of healing) with good views of the other temples.

What to See

Above: *compact Portovenere on the Ligurian coast*
Right: signora *of the late 20th century*

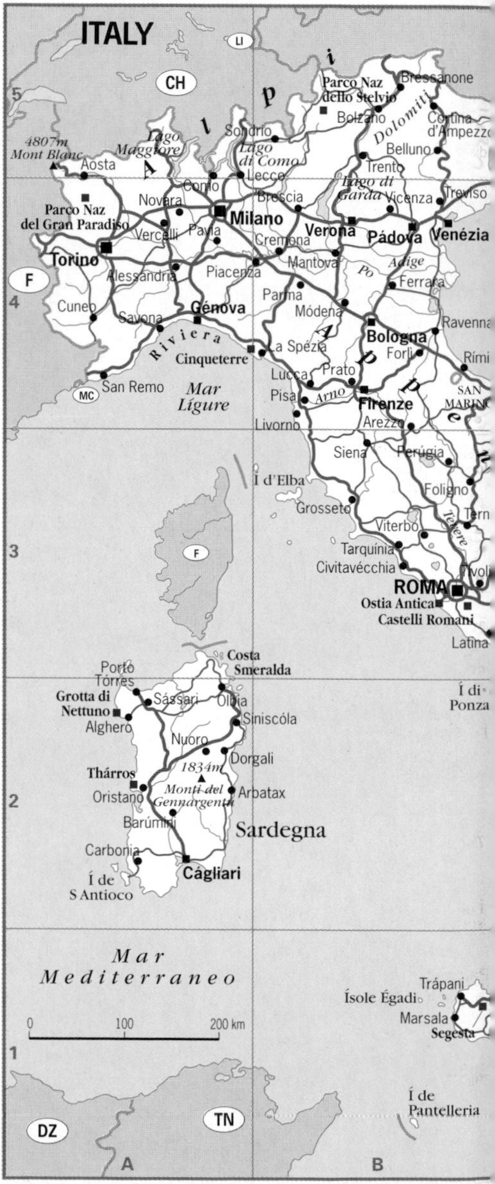

ITALY
LI
CH
Alpi
Parco Naz dello Stelvio
Bressanone
Bolzano
Dolomiti
Cortina d'Ampezzo
4807m Mont Blanc
Lago Maggiore
Sondrio
Lago di Como
Belluno
Aosta
Lecco
Trento
Como
Lago di Garda
Vicenza
Treviso
Parco Naz del Gran Paradiso
Novara
Brescia
Milano
Vercelli
Pavia
Verona
Pádova
Venézia
Torino
Cremona
Mantova
Adige
Alessandria
Piacenza
Po
Ferrara
F
Parma
Cuneo
Génova
Módena
Savona
Appennini
Bologna
Ravenna
Riviera
La Spézia
Cinqueterre
Forlì
Rímini
Lucca
Prato
San Remo
Mar Lígure
Pisa
Arno
Firenze
SAN MARINO
MC
Livorno
Arezzo
Siena
Perúgia
Í d'Elba
Foligno
Grosseto
Tevere
Terni
F
Viterbo
Tarquínia
Civitavécchia
Tivoli
ROMA
Ostia Antica
Castelli Romani
Latina
Costa Smeralda
Porto Tórres
Grotta di Nettuno
Sássari
Olbia
Í di Ponza
Alghero
Siniscóla
Nuoro
Dorgali
1834m
Thárros
Monti del Gennargentu
Arbatax
Oristano
Barúmini
Sardegna
Carbonia
Cágliari
Í de S Antioco
Mar Mediterraneo
Trápani
Ísole Égadi
0 100 200 km
Marsala
Segesta
Í de Pantelleria
DZ
TN
A
B
1
2
3
4
5

- F France
- CH Switzerland
- LI Liechtenstein
- A Austria
- SLO Slovenia
- H Hungary
- HR Croatia
- BIH Bosnia-Herzegovina
- YU Yugoslavia
- AL Albania
- DZ Algeria
- TN Tunisia

Northwest Italy

Here tiny remote mountain villages clinging to the foothills of the Alps seem to belong to a different world from the sophisticated cities of Milan and Turin, the fashionable resorts of the Riviera and the Lakes, and the historic splendour of medieval and Renaissance towns such as Mantua and Cremona. The majestic mountains, the seemingly endless plains and the picture-postcard coasts of northwest Italy provide winter and summer sports that include skiing, mountaineering, swimming and sailing, and vast areas of unspoiled natural charm. Then there are fantastic art collections and historic monuments, excellent cuisine, and superb *alta moda* shopping. In spite of all this natural and historic beauty, the northwest is also where many of Italy's most important industries and businesses are based, making it among the richest and most productive areas of Europe.

'Before the golden statue on the summit of Milan's cathedral spire was lost in the blue sky, the Alps, stupendously confused in lofty peaks and ridges, clouds and snow, were towering in our path.'

CHARLES DICKENS,
Pictures from Italy, 1845

Milano (Milan)

What Rome, Florence and Venice are to romantic, historic Italy, Milan is to stylish, modern Italy. This busy metropolis is Italy's second-biggest city and, while Rome is the political capital, Milan can claim to be the capital of business, finance and industry. For most visitors Milan means chic Italian fashion, stylish bars and restaurants, bustling streets filled with smartly dressed locals brandishing *telefonini*, and the chance of seeing opera in the world-famous Teatro alla Scala (► 112). However, there is even more to Milan, and the city also boasts some splendid art collections and monuments.

Galleria Vittorio Emanuele II: the essence of modern Milan

What to See in Milan

CASTELLO SFORZESCO ✪✪

The castle is basically 15th century with some later additions. It was the seat of the Sforza family, the dukes of Milan, until the late 19th century when it first housed the city's collections of art, applied arts, archaeology and coins. Among the highlights are Michelangelo's unfinished sculpture, the *Pietà Rondanini*, and pictures by Mantegna, Bellini and Tiepolio; the Museo degli Strumenti Musicali (Musical Instruments Museum); and a collection of 18th- and 19th-century costumes.

- 28A4
- Piazza Castello
- 02 875 851
- Daily 9–5:30. Closed Mon, public hols
- Few
- Lanza
- Free

GALLERIA D'ARTE MODERNA (GALLERY OF MODERN ART) ✪

This gallery of modern art was opened in 1984 in the Villa Reale and is expanding. The emphasis is on talian artists of the 20th century. Foreign artists are also well represented.

- Villa Reale, Via Palestro 16
- 02 7600 2819
- Tue–Sat 9:30–5:30. Closed public hols
- Good
- Palestro
- Free

DUOMO (► 19, TOP TEN)

GALLERIA VITTORIO EMANUELE II ✪✪

This luxurious 19th-century shopping arcade is packed with sophisticated shops, bars and restaurants. Look out for the zodiac floor mosaics and representations of Europe, America, Africa and Asia under the impressive, airy glass dome.

- Piazza del Duomo and Piazza della Scala
- Duomo

PINACOTECA AMBROSIANA

Piazza Pio XI 2
02 806 921
Tue–Sun 10–5:30. Closed public hols
Cordusio
Expensive

The *palazzo* was built in 1609 to house Cardinal Federico Borromeo's art collection and 30,000-volume library. An immaculate restoration job (1990–97), costing 45 billion *lire* (well over £15 million), has returned it to its original splendour. The paintings from the 14th to 19th centuries include works by Caravaggio, Raphael, Tiepolo, Titian and Giorgone. Special exhibitions occasionally feature some of the library's major manuscripts, which include a 5th-century illustrated *Iliad*, an early edition of Dante's *Commedia Divina* and Leonardo's Atlantic Codex.

PINACOTECA DI BRERA

Via Brera 28
02 722 631
Tue–Sun 8:30–7
Lanza
Few
Moderate

Milan's most important art gallery is housed in a 17th-century *palazzo* which became the Accademia di Belle Arti in the 18th century. Unlike many other Italian collections, this one includes later artists, among them Modigliani, Morandi, Picasso and Braque, as well as the 19th-century Italians, Francesco Hayez and Giovanni Fattori. But earlier periods are particularly well represented too, with masterpieces by Bramante, Caravaggio, Raphael, Canaletto, Van Dyck and Rubens; notable is Mantegna's *Dead Christ,* in which the artist makes disturbingly dramatic use of an unusual perspective.

SANTA MARIA DELLE GRAZIE

Piazza Santa Maria delle Grazie 2
02 498 7588
Tue–Sun 8:15–6:45
Cadorna
Few Expensive

Bramante contributed to this attractive late 15th-century monastery by designing the dome, gallery and cloisters. The gem, however, is in the nearby refectory, where Leonardo da Vinci frescoed his much reproduced *Cenacolo* (*Last Supper*) on the north wall, between 1485 and 1497. Being a perfectionist, he never quite finished it; but more tragically, over the centuries the ravages of time, damp and warfare have taken their toll and the painting has deteriorated badly. It is nevertheless still spectacular.

Santa Maria delle Grazie in Milan

What to See in Northwest Italy

AOSTA ✪

The 'Rome of the Alps' is surrounded by stupendous mountains at the crossroads between the Mont Blanc and St Bernard tunnels. Although mainly used as a holiday-makers' stopover on the way to the Alps, it has an interesting centre with ancient Roman remains. These date back to the 1st century BC, when the city was founded as *Augusta Praetoria*, and include a theatre, an amphitheatre, a forum and the Arco di Augusto.

28A5
Piazza Chanoux 8
0165 236 627; www.regione.vda.it/turismo

CINQUETERRE ✪✪

One of the wildest stretches of the Ligurian coastline gets its name from five picturesque villages that cling to cliff edges and tumble down steep hillsides into pretty little bays. Although all the villages can be reached by train, only two of them are easily accessible by road – **Monterosso al Mare**, which is the largest of the Cinqueterre and has the biggest, busiest beaches, and Riomaggiore. Between lie Vernazza, founded by the Romans in a sheltered cove, and Corniglia and Manarola which have wonderful views over the sea. All are linked by steep footpaths.

28A4

Monterosso al Mare
Via Fegina
0187 817 5060; www.laspezia.it

Below: *boats lie at rest in the ancient harbour of Vernazza, still a working fishing port*

CREMONA ✪

This is an important, agricultural market town with a strong musical tradition. As well as being the birthplace of composer Claudio Monteverdi (1567–1643), Cremona was where the first violins were made, in the 16th century, and where Antonio Stradivari (1644–1737), or 'Stradivarius' – the most famous violin-maker of all time – had his workshop. His drawings, models and violins can be seen in the **Museo Stradivariano**. The magnificent Romanesque-Gothic Duomo (1107–1332) is flanked by the 112m Torrazzo tower with its 15th-century astronomical clock.

28B4

Museo Stradivariano
Via Palestro 17
0372 461 886
Tue–Sat 8:30–6, Sun and hols 10–6. Closed 1Jan, 1 May and 25 Dec
Few
Moderate

GENOVA (GENOA)

28A4

Duomo San Lorenzo
Piazza San Lorenzo
010 345 0048; Museo del Tesoro: 010 247 1831
Museo: Mon–Sat 9–12, 3–6 (guided tours only)
Moderate

Aquarium
Ponte Spinola
010 248 1205
Mon–Wed and Fri 9:30–7:30, Thu 9:30AM–11PM, Sat, Sun 9:30– 8:30. Closed Mon, Nov–Feb

The birthplace of Christopher Columbus, Genoa has been an important maritime centre since the 11th century, and today its bustling, modern harbours form Italy's most important commercial port. The square 117m-high lighthouse, called the *Lanterna* (renovated 1547), used to burn wood to guide ships into port, and the modern aquarium houses an exciting collection of sea plant and animal life in reconstructed natural habitats. Behind the Porto Vecchio is the **Duomo (San Lorenzo)**, a mix of architectural styles from Romanesque to baroque, with a fine collection of relics in its Museo del Tesoro. Among the most interesting palaces in the city, the Palazzi Bianco and Rosso, on the splendid Via Garibaldi, house important art collections, while the recently restored Palazzo del Principe gives an insight into how the aristocratic Doria family lived.

LAGO MAGGIORE

28A5
Boats on the lake and to the islands from Verbania

Palazzo Borromeo
Isola Bella
0323 30 556
Apr–Oct
Moderate

This long, mountain-encircled lake runs up into Switzerland. Although some stretches of its banks are overdeveloped, other parts offer the most romantic of idealised lakeside scenery. The lake's most breathtaking feature are the three Isole Borromee, owned by the Borromeo family. On Isola Bella, the 17th-century Carlo Borromeo III built a luxurious palace with spectacular gardens for his wife Isabella. Isola dei Pescatori has an attractive village on it, while Isola Madre is covered in gardens. On the lake's shores stand the attractive towns of Angera, Baveno, Cannero Riviera and Verbania (its main centre), holiday destinations since Victorian times.

Above: *Genoa's royal palace*

Lago di Como

This drive is best avoided at weekends in summer when the roads are particularly crowded.

From Lecco (birthplace of the author Alessandro Manzoni, 1785–1873) cross the River Adda and take statale 583 up the western shore of the lake as far as Onno.

Here you leave the lake, following the road to Valbrona, which has wonderful views west to the Grigne mountains.

Distance
183km

Time
A full day without much time for stops, but nearly all of the route affords marvellous views

Start/end point
Lecco
28A5

The road meanders through Asso, Lasnigo (with its Romanesque church of S. Alessandro) and Civenna to Bellagio, between the 'legs' of the lake.

Bellagio is one of the most attractive of the lakeside resorts with pretty views, narrow streets and elegant villas.

From here rejoin statale 583 and follow it along the lake shore through Nesso and Torno to Como.

The historic buildings here include a Gothic-Renaissance Duomo and aristocratic villas from the 18th to early 20th centuries, when Lake Como was one of Europe's most chic holiday destinations.

From Como take scenic statale 340 along the lake's western shore past Cernobbio, Torrigia and Argegno.

From Sala Argegno you can see Lake Como's only island, Isola Comacina. Next come Ossuccio, whose church of Santa Maria Maddalena has a Gothic bell-tower, and Tremezzo, where the gardens of Villa Carlotta are particularly spectacular in springtime.

Lunch
Santo Stefano (€€)
Piazza XI Febbraio 3, Lenno (about 27km from Como on statale 340)
0344 55 434
Closed Mon

The road from here hugs the lake shore up to the quieter, wilder reaches of the lake. At the northern tip stay on statale 340 when it turns back south. You can continue back to Lecco on the scenic old, lakeside route, or take the faster, new statale 36, which goes through many tunnels as far as Abbadia Lariana.

Above: *an alternative to driving round Lake Como would be a tour by boat on its peaceful waters*

Far right: overview of the city of Turin: a gracious centre contrasts with less pleasing industrial parts

Right: *marching columns in the colonnade of Mantua's mighty ducal palace*

28B4

Palazzo Ducale
- Piazza Sordello
- 0376 382 150
- Tue–Sun 8:45–7:15. Closed 1 Jan, 1 May, 25 Dec
- Few
- Expensive

MANTOVA (MANTUA)

Looking like the set for a somewhat lugubrious medieval period film, Mantua's historic centre is surrounded on three sides by water, giving it an occasionally dank climate. That said, the town has a wonderfully historic atmosphere and some magnificent treasures. It was also the birthplace of the poet Virgil. First among its main sights is the titanic **Palazzo Ducale**, home to the ruling Gonzaga family whose frescoed portraits by local painter Mantegna (1431–1505) can be seen in the Camera degli Sposi. The same family's Palazzo del Tè was designed and sumptuously decorated by Giulio Romano in 1525–35. Romano was also responsible for the stuccoes inside the Duomo, while the façade of the Basilica di Sant'Andrea is the work of the pioneer Renaissance architect Alberti (1404–72).

28A4

Certosa di Pavia
- Viale del Monumento
- 0382 925 613
- May–Sep, Tue–Sun 9–11:30, 2:30–6 (Oct–Apr closes at sunset)
- Certosa station
- Few
- Donation

PAVIA

Throughout history, Pavia has been an important centre. As capital of the Lombard kings until 1359, it hosted the coronation of, among others, Charlemagne in 774. During the Middle Ages and the Renaissance its ancient 11th-century university could boast such alumni as Petrarch and Leonardo da Vinci. While the town itself is not short of impressive historic sights, Pavia's main sight lies a few kilometres north. The **Certosa di Pavia** (Charterhouse of Pavia) was founded in 1396 although most of the present buildings date from the 15th and 16th centuries. Behind a well-proportioned and exquisitely carved Renaissance façade, the interior is mainly Gothic adorned with marquetry, frescoes and sculpture. In the first chapel on the left is an altarpiece by Perugino, flanked by works by Bergognone, who also painted frescoes in the transept. Some of the altars include semiprecious stones.

RIVIERA LIGURE

From Ventimiglia in the west to La Spezia in the east, with Genoa (➤ 34) in the middle, the Ligurian coast is known as the Riviera Ligure. The towns and resorts along this stretch cover a range of styles and tastes from the fishing-village charm of the Cinqueterre (➤ 33), through historic Cervo, Albenga, Rapallo and Portovenere to the revamped 19th-century aristocratic exuberance of San Remo. Near the French border is **Villa Hanbury**, with gardens of exotic plants first laid out by English botanist Sir Thomas Hanbury in the 1860s and 70s. East of Genoa is the chic sailing resort of Portofino, on a peninsula.

28A4

Villa Hanbury

Corso Monte Carlo 43, Località

0184 229 507

Mid-Jun to Sep 9–6; Apr to mid-Jun, Oct, 10–5; Nov–Mar, 10–4. Closed Wed Nov–Mar

Few

Expensive

TORINO (TURIN)

This solemn northern city combines its role as the capital of the Italian motor industry with being a city of art and, most famously, home of the Turin Shroud. The latter is kept in the Capella della Sacra Sindone, next to the 15th-century **Duomo** and, although it is rarely on show, it continues to attract the faithful.

The nearby Palazzo Reale, former residence of the Savoy royal family, contains many artistic treasures. Other sights include the Palazzo dell'Accademia delle Scienze, which houses the Galleria Sabauda painting collection and the important Egyptian museum; the splendid façade of the Palazzo Carignano, united Italy's first parliament building; and the elegant main shopping street, Via Roma.

28A4

Aeroporto Caselle

Duomo

Piazza San Giovanni

011 436 1540

Did you know ?

The Fabbrica Italiana Automobili Torino (FIAT) was founded in 1899 and soon became one of the largest businesses in Europe. Today, having expanded and bought several other Italian car manufacturers, it accounts for nearly 80 per cent of the cars made in Italy. The owner of Fiat, Gianni Agnelli, now also owns Italy's most famous football team, Juventus.

In the Know

If you only have a short time to visit Italy, or would like to get a real flavour of the country, here are some ideas:

10 Ways to Be a Local

Use bars for a quick *caffè* standing at the *banco* or a leisurely *cappuccino* sitting at an outside table.
Learn a few words of Italian – it always goes down well.
Don't hurry – stroll rather than stride.
Eat properly – pasta is a *primo* that comes *before* the main course (*secondo*) and not a meal in itself.
Finish dinner with black coffee and a *digestivo*.
Always carry sunglasses and wear them; it's not just a pose – the sun can be painfully strong, even in winter.
Enjoy men's attention and compliments if you are a woman, rather than be offended by them. Be politely assertive if you don't reciprocate the interest.
Dress comfortably but not scruffily; Italians are nearly always well turned out.
Enjoy the wines but don't get drunk; Italians seldom do.
Be flexible – what you don't do today, you can do tomorrow or the next day.

10 Good Places to Have Lunch

Cecilia Metella (€€) ✉ Via Appia Antica 117/119, Rome ☎ 06 511 0213. Evocative shady garden with fountains and statues.
Certosa di Maggiano (€€€) ✉ Via Certosa 82, Siena ☎ 0577 288 180. Tuscan cuisine in a delightful setting in an old monastery.
CraccoPeck (€€€) ✉ Via Victor Hugo 4, Milano ☎ 02 876 774. Work up a good appetite to do justice to this elegant food-lover's paradise, with service and a wine list to match the excellent menu.
Don Alfonso (€€€) ✉ Corso Sant'Agata 11/13, Sant'Agata Sui Due Golfi, Naples ☎ 081 878 0026. One of the best restaurants in the south with an excellent *menu degustazione* (➤ 95)
Frantoio (€€€) ✉ Via Cavour 21, Lerici, La Spezia ☎ 0187 964 174. Best of Ligurian sea specialities in the heart of this pretty old town south of the Cinqueterre.
Locanda Cipriani, Torcello, Venice (➤ 45)
Porta al Cassero (€€) ✉ Via Porta al Cassero, Montalcino, Tuscany ☎ 0577 847 196. Simple and not-so-simple Tuscan specialities in the heart of the town that produces Brunello di Montalcino (➤ 69).
Sandro al Navile (€€€) ✉ Via del Sostegno 15, Bologna ☎ 051 634 3100. Good example of the cuisine of one of Italy's gastronomic capitals.
Sora Margherita (€) ✉ Piazza delle Cinque Scole 30, Rome ☎ 06 686 4002. Genuine home cooking in a traditional trattoria in the Roman Ghetto.

City Italians dress for the street, not the beach

Temptation (€€€) ✉ Via Torretta 94, Località Sferracavallo, Palermo ☎ 091 691 1104. A fixed-menu fish restaurant around the *piazza* of this bustling little Sicilian fishing village.

10 Top Activities

- Looking at art
- Eating (see above, ➤ 68–9 and 92–9)
- Going to the beach
- Skiing (➤ 115)
- Opera and outdoor concerts (➤ 110–112)
- Walking and trekking in the mountains (➤ 12–13, 115)
- Religion: see the Pope at St Peter's (➤ 16) every Wed morning. During the summer he's at Castel Gandolfo (➤ 80, 116)
- Football (➤ 115)
- Shopping for designer labels (➤ 105–7)
- Hanging out in bars, parks or any other public place

Piazzas

Brà, Verona, for its Roman amphitheatre (➤ 51)
del Campo, Siena, for its theatricality (➤ 66)
Campo dei Miracoli, Pisa, for its surreal sense of order (➤ 64)
del Duomo, Milan, for a piece of Gothic in downtown Milan (➤ 19)
del Duomo, Lecce, for its delicacy (➤ 22)
Navona, Rome, for its fountains and vastness (➤ 78)
San Carlo, Turin, for cool, baroque elegance
San Marco, Venice; the most famous square in the world (➤ 23)
dei Signori, Vicenza, for Palladian *palazzi* (➤ 51)
della Signoria, Florence, for its breathtaking art (➤ 55)

5 Best Frescoes

- Cappella degli Scrovegni, Padua, by Giotto (➤ 48)
- Cappella Sistina, Rome, by Michelangelo (➤ 17)
- San Francesco, Arezzo, by Piero della Francesca (➤ 57)
- Santa Maria del Carmini, Florence, by Masaccio (➤ 56)
- Santa Maria della Grazie, Milan, by Leonardo (➤ 32)

In St Mark's Square, Venice: a breathing space in the busy round of sightseeing

Places to Go to the Beach

Costiera Calabrese (➤ 86), for relatively undeveloped bays between cliffs.
Isole Eolie off Sicily (➤ 13), for wild beauty (although they're busy in summer).
Riviera di Liguria (➤ 37), for fishing villages with a veneer of sophistication.
Salentino (➤ 88), for sandy beaches where you really can get away from it all.
Sardinia (➤ 89), for beaches that cover the gamut from jet-set to deserted and reachable only by boat.

Many Italians still favour the moped for buzzing around the narrow streets

Northeast Italy

Most people come to northeast Italy to see Venice (➤ 42–5), whose magnetic charm attracts about 12 million tourists every year. However, there are plenty of other things to see and do in this scenically varied area, which stretches from the majestic, rocky Dolomites to the seemingly unending flatness of the Po Valley. For a start, its cuisine, particularly that of the Emilia Romagna region, is renowned throughout Italy. Medieval prosperity, often based on trade with the East, has left a heritage of churches and imposing civic buildings. They complement the stately palaces, elegant villas and priceless art collections of the powerful families and prince-bishops who ruled the area throughout much of its history and attracted some of the greatest artistic and architectural geniuses of all time.

‘Of all dreamy delights, that of floating in a gondola along the canals and out on the Lagoon is surely the greatest’

GEORGE ELIOT,
Journal, 1860

More than 100 palazzi *line Venice's Grand Canal*

Venezia (Venice)

One of the most painted, filmed and written about cities in the world, Venice is disturbingly beautiful; nothing quite prepares you for that first glimpse of distant domes and spires emerging from the flat, grey waters like a mirage. Within the city, murky canal water laps the bases of dreamlike buildings, creating a slightly disorienting, rocking effect enhanced by the gentle rattle of the wind in boats and mooring poles. Behind the canals lie tiny, winding alleys in which even the best map-reader soon gets lost and all sense of urgency has to be forgotten.

What to See in Venice

GALLERIA DELL'ACCADEMIA ✪✪✪

28B4
Campo della Carità
041 522 2247
Tue–Sun 8:15–7:15, Mon 8:15–2. Closed 1 Jan, 1 May, 25 Dec
Few
Expensive

This is the place to see Venetian art from the 14th to 18th centuries. While 14th-century artists (such as the Veneziano brothers) reflect the Byzantine and International Gothic movements that swept Europe, from the Renaissance onwards Venetian artists (such as Giorgione, Lotto, Titian, Tintoretto and Veronese) developed a style that made greater use of colour and softer, more sensuous lines than their contemporaries elsewhere were using.

CA' D'ORO (GOLDEN HOUSE) ✪✪✪

Calle Ca' d'Oro
041 523 8790
Tue–Sun 8:15–7:15, Mon 8:15–2. Closed 1 Jan, 1 May, 25 Dec
Cheap

Regarded as the most beautiful *palazzo* in Venice, the lacy, Gothic façade of this stately residence (built 1422–40), used to be richly decorated with gold leaf and other luxurious materials. Now it houses the Galleria Giorgio Franchetti, the musician's spectacular collection of sculpture, tapestry and painting, which was donated to the state in 1916.

MADONNA DELL'ORTO ✪

Campo Madonna dell'Orto
041 719 933
Daily 10–5
Cheap

Inside this pretty 15th-century Gothic church are the tomb of Tintoretto and some fine examples of his work. Most noteworthy of the paintings are a dramatic *Last Judgement* (to the right of the chancel) and an *Adoration of the Golden Calf*, on the left.

A gondola is the romantic way to travel on the Grand Canal, but you see just as much from a river boat

Canale Grande

Venice's main thoroughfare is the Grand Canal which – instead of taxis, buses and cars – is thronged with gondolas, riverbuses and motor launches. Its sides are lined with aristocratic *palazzi*, ranging in condition from crisply restored and maintained to melancholy, crumbling and neglected.

Leaving from San Marco Vallareso, past Harry's Bar (right) and the imposing 17th-century customs house (left), you see the baroque church of Santa Maria della Salute (left) followed by the coloured marble façade of the Palazzo Dario (1487). Shortly before the wooden Accademia footbridge (1932) is Palazzo Barbaro (right) where Monet, Whistler and Henry James all stayed. Beyond the bridge, on the right, is the Accademia (see opposite).

Just beyond the riverbus stop is Browning's former home, Ca' Rezzonico (right), now a museum of 18th-century Venice. The next bridge, the Rialto (1591), has shops up the middle; round the corner is the pescheria (fish market) on the left and Ca' d'Oro (see opposite) on the right.

Further on are baroque Ca'Pesaro (left), the baroque church of San Stae (left), the magnificent Renaissance Palazzo Vendramin Calergi (right), where Wagner died in 1883, and the 17th-century Fondaco dei Turchi warehouses. The third and final bridge is Ponte dei Scalzi.

Distance
Nearly 4km

Time
About 40 mins by public riverbus (No 1 stops at every stop, No 82 stops at only six). You can hire a water-taxi (which will be quicker) or a gondola (which will be much slower and very expensive), or take one of the organised tours from the Riva degli Schiavoni near Piazza San Marco.

Start point
San Marco Vallareso riverbus stop

End point
Ferrovia riverbus stop

Lunch
Alla Frasca (€)
✉ Cannaregio, 5176 Campiello della Carità. (Take riverbus 52, alight at Fondamenta Nuove)
☎ 041 528 5433
🕐 Closed Thu and two weeks in Aug

PIAZZA SAN MARCO (➤ 23, TOP TEN)

- Campo dei Frari
- Mon–Sat 9–6, Sun and public hols 1–6
- Cheap

SANTA MARIA GLORIOSA DEI FRARI ✪✪

This sprawling Gothic church is packed with masterpieces by famous artists. Among them are a Donatello statue of John the Baptist (1450) to the right of the altar, a Bellini altarpiece in the sacristry, Titian's *Assumption of the Virgin* (1518) above the main altar, and Pietro Lombardo's carved rood-screen (1475). Among the many tombs and memorials are Canova's surprising pyramidical tomb (1822) based on one of his own designs, and a memorial to Titian.

- Campo Santi Giovanni e Paolo
- Mon–Sat 7:30–12:30, 3–7:15, Sun 2–6:30
- Cheap

SANTI GIOVANNI E PAOLO ✪✪✪

Also known as San Zanipolo, this severe 14th-century Dominican church made the perfect setting for the Doges' funerals. They were held here from 1450 and the church contains many of their tombs. Among the most interesting of these are those by Pietro Lombardo, especially the arched tomb of Andrea Vendramin (1476–8), to the left of the altar. Other gems here include a magnificent polyptych by Bellini (1465), to the right of the entrance, and works by Veronese. The equestrian statue of Bartolomeo Colleoni (1480s) in the piazza outside is by Andrea Verrocchio.

Doge Giovanni Mocenigo, 15th-century ruler of Venice, by Gentile Bellini

- Campo San Rocco
- 041 523 4864
- Apr–Oct 9–5:30; Nov–Mar 10–4. Closed 1 Jan, Easter, 25 Dec
- Few
- Expensive; free 16 Aug (Saint's Day)

SCUOLA GRANDE DI SAN ROCCO ✪✪✪

Anyone with any interest in Tintoretto should visit this building, erected in 1515–49 to house a charitable confraternity. Its two floors contain more than 50 Tintoretto paintings executed from 1564 to 1587 and including some of his greatest works, such as the sombre *Crucifixion* (1565) and eight scenes from the Life of the Virgin (1583–7). There are a few works by other artists, including Titian and the sculptor Francesco Pianta, whose caricature bust of Tintoretto in the upper hall is recognisable from the master's own self-portrait at the entrance to the Sala dell'Albergo.

Venezia Islands

In the Lagoon north of Venice is an archipelago of flat little islands. Many of these are uninhabited or privately owned, but some have been populated for centuries. Three – Merano, Burano and Torcello, each in a different way, are interesting places to visit on a day trip from Venice.

Distance
20km

Time
Allow about 2½–3 hours without stops; up to a day with stops

Start/end point
San Zaccharia

Lunch
Locanda Cipriani (€€€)
Piazza S Fosca 29, Torcello
041 730 150
Closed Tue and Jan

From San Zaccharia the boat heads southeast past the island of San Giorgio Maggiore.

The church here (1559–80), by Palladio, contains works by Tintoretto and has excellent views from its dome.

The boat then chugs round the eastern peninsula of Venice before heading northwest, past the Isola di San Michele.

The island has been used as a graveyard since the 19th century; Diaghilev, Stravinsky and Ezra Pound are among those who lie behind its protective walls.

North of here is the island of Murano.

The centre of Venetian glass-blowing since the 13th century, Murano has numerous factories, offering guided tours, and the Museo Vetrario with glass pieces from the 15th century onwards.

Next comes the island of Burano.

Once a great lace-making centre, Burano is now more remarkable for its psychedelic, painted houses and the leaning tower of San Martino church.

Torcello, the last island, is the most historic.

Torcello was once a thriving community of 20,000, but started to decline in the 14th century. Now all that remain are two adjoining churches set in serene rural scenery near an old canal. The 9th- to 11th-century Cathedral of Santa Maria Assunta has a charmingly expressive mosaic of the Last Judgement, while the 12th-century church of Santa Fosca is surrounded on three sides by a harmonious peristyle and has a tranquil, simple interior.

Palladio's influential church of San Giorgio Maggiore's harmonious design is based on mathematical principles

What to See in Northeast Italy

28B4
Aeroporto Marconi

San Giacomo Maggiore
Piazza Rossini
051 225 970
Apr–Oct, 10–1, 3–7; Nov–Mar, 10–1, 2–8
Donation

Pinacoteca Nazionale
Via delle Belle Arti 56
051 243 222
Tue–Sat 9–2 (Thu 9–7), Sun 9–1. Closed public hols
Moderate

Abbazia di Santo Stefano
Via Santo Stefano
051 223 256
Mon–Sat 9–12, 3:30–6; Sun and public hols 9–1, 3:30–6:30

BOLOGNA ✪✪✪

The capital of Emilia Romagna is a cultured, prosperous city of arcaded streets and historic monuments. It has one of the oldest universities in Europe (13th century or earlier) which numbers the inventor of radio, Guglielmo Marconi, among its alumni. In the heart of Bologna is the Piazza del Nettuno, with a magnificent Neptune fountain (1566) sculpted by Giambologna. The Basilica di San Petronio (started in 1390) has a spacious, calm interior with high, vaulted ceilings and exquisite biblical bas-relief doors (1425–38) by Jacopo della Quercia. Opposite is the Renaissance Palazzo del Podestà. To the east are two 12th-century *torri pendenti* (leaning towers), survivors of the nearly 200 towers built in the Middle Ages by local nobles. The nearby church of **San Giacomo Maggiore** contains the magnificent chapel of the Bentivoglio family, with frescoes, paintings and della Quercia's Bentivoglio tomb (1435). The **Pinacoteca Nazionale** has in its important collection works by Bolognese painters Guido Reni, Guercino and the Carracci. Also worth a visit is the **Abbazia di Santo Stefano**, a complex of four medieval churches dating for the most part from the 11th century.

Drama at dusk in Bologna's central square: the Neptune fountain with its bold bronze figure of the sea god

28B5
Via Stazione 9 0472 836 401; www.brixen.org

BRESSANONE ✪✪

Known as Brixen by its German-speaking population, this delightful medieval Alpine town lies on the road to Austria and is well placed for hillwalkers and lovers of mountain scenery. Until 1803 it was ruled by a prince-bishop whose sumptuous palace (rebuilt in 1595 over a 14th-century original) now houses a museum of art and local history. The 18th-century Duomo has a beautiful 13th-century cloister with 15th-century frescoes.

DOLOMITI (DOLOMITES)

Right up in the north of Italy, nestling under Austria, is the German-speaking Alto Adige (or Südtirol), much of it covered by the Dolomite mountains, which look as though they've been carved, folded and squeezed into an extraordinary variety of gnarled crags. Although this is Italy, the language, scenery, architecture and much of the culture are strongly influenced by Austria, and nearly all the place names have versions in German. The capital of Alto Adige is Bolzano (or Bozen), which has a fine 15th-century Gothic Duomo, and the **Museo Archeologico dell'Alto Adige**, where the highlight is the 5,300 year-old mummified corpse of what was probably a murder victim. To the west of this is a string of mountain resorts from which cable-cars carry skiers in winter, hillwalkers in summer and view-seekers all year round up into the 2,300–3,300m-high mountains.

28B5
To Bolzano, then buses to other centres

Museo Archeologico dell'Alto Adige

Via Museo 43
0471 982 098; www.iceman.it
Tue–Sun 10–6 (Thu 10–8). Closed 1 Jan, 1 May, 25 Dec
Expensive

Above: *the Rifugio Locatelli offers rest and refreshment among the peaks of the Dolomites*

FERRARA

This evocative old walled town, ruled by the rich and powerful Este family for centuries, is slightly off the beaten tourist track. The historic centre, with its Renaissance grid layout, contains some marvellous buildings. Chief among these are a 12th-century **Duomo** with a spectacular arched façade showing scenes from the Last Judgement, and **Castello Estense** (started 1385), the fairytale moated seat of the Este family, whose rivals were left to rot in its chilling dungeons. Among the most beautiful *palazzi* are Palazzo Schifanoia, another Este residence, started in 1385 and with murals by local painters, and Palazzo dei Diamanti, now an art gallery and museum. In winter, dense white mists rise up from the nearby River Po and smother the entire area.

28B4
Castello Estense
0532 209 370

Duomo

Piazza Comunale
0532 761 299
Museum: Tue–Sun 9:30–2. Closed public hols
Donation

Castello Estense

Largo Castello
Tue–Sun 9:30–5. Closed 25 Dec
Moderate

28B4

Palazzo dei Musei

Largo di Porta Sant'Agostino 337

Galleria: 059 439 5711; Biblioteca: 059 222 248

Galleria: Tue–Sun 8:30–7; Biblioteca: Mon–Thu 8:30–7, Fri 8:30–3:30, Sat 8:30–1. Closed public hols

Few

Moderate

MODENA

Founded as the Roman colony of Mutina, Modena has flourished throughout much of its history and is now associated with those symbols of modern prosperity, Ferrari and Maserati cars, which are manufactured in its outskirts. Among the principal sights of its winding medieval streets and pretty piazzas is a particularly fine Romanesque Duomo (started in 1099), with an 88m-high Gothic tower, La Ghirlandina. On its west façade are 12th-century reliefs by Wiligelmo (one of the first named artists in Italy); inside, the rood-screen has scenes from the Passion. Within the **Palazzo dei Musei** is the massive Este Biblioteca (library) of rare, historic manuscripts and the family's collection of works by mainly local artists.

28B4

Cappella degli Scrovegni

Piazza Ermitani

049 201 0020; www.padovanet.it/museicivici

Daily 9–7. Closed public hols. By appointment only (at least 72 hours in advance)

Good

Expensive

PADOVA (PADUA)

This stately old university town has a matchless collection of historic and artistic treasures. Top of the list comes the **Cappella degli Scrovegni**, an early 14th-century building plastered with Giotto's elegant, soothing frescoes of scenes from the Life of Christ. Reopened in March 2002 after extensive restoration, this now has a draconian admission procedure for visitors (see left). Around the altar of the 13th-century Basilica di Sant'Antonio are Donatello's bronze reliefs of the saint's life (1444). The Donatello statue of the *condottiere* (mercenary soldier) Gattamelata, outside, is the first equestrian statue of the Renaissance. Other gems include the Chiesa and Museo degli Eremitani, both packed with priceless Renaissance art and historic artefacts, including two frescoes by Mantegna, the only ones to survive a bombing raid in 1944; the 16th-century anatomy theatre in the University's Palazzo del Bo; Titian's first known works in the Scuola del Santo; and the 16th-century Duomo, designed by Michelangelo.

Padua's Prato della Valle: this wooded square, laid out in the 18th century, is encircled by a canal

PARMA ✪✪

Not only is Parma one of the eating capitals of Italy, but it also has some fine buildings and works of art. The main cupola of the text-book Romanesque Duomo is covered with Correggio's *Assumption* (1534), while in the south transept is a 12th-century frieze showing the Descent from the Cross. Perpendicular to the Duomo is an exquisite 16-sided baptistery (1196, by Benedetto Antelami), with unrivalled 13th-century reliefs and frescoes depicting the Life of Christ. The **Galleria Nazionale** has a fine collection of 14th- to 18th-century art.

28B4

Galleria Nazionale

Piazzale della Pilotta 15

0521 233 309

Tue–Sun 9–2. Closed 1 Jan, 1 May and 25 Dec

Expensive

Did you know ?

The creation of Parma's two most famous products, ham and cheese, is closely linked. The firm, flavoursome Parmigiano *(Parmesan) cheese is made using techniques that are centuries old and the resulting whey is fed to pigs whose meat is then air-cured for several months to produce the sweet, raw* prosciutto *(ham).*

RAVENNA (➤ 25, TOP TEN)

RIMINI ✪

The bustling seafront of one of Italy's most popular resorts hides an interesting and attractive historic centre which is based around Piazza Cavour and the 14th-century Palazzo del Podestà. The most important monument is the church, the Tempio Malestiano, designed in 1450 by early Renaissance architect Lon Battista Alberti.

28B4

Above: *the frescoed vault of the baptistery in Parma*

TRENTO ✪✪

Famous for the Council of Trent (1545–63), when senior Catholic churchmen met to discuss their reaction to the threat of Protestantism, this attractive town is surrounded by mountains. Its Romanesque-Gothic Duomo was where the Council's decrees were proclaimed. Piazza del Duomo contains the medieval Palazzo Pretorio and some 16th-century frescoed houses. The magnificent **Castello del Buonconsiglio** has frescoes by Romanino and others, and houses part of the province's art collection.

28B5

Castello del Buonconsiglio

Via Bernardo Clesio

0461 233 770

Tue–Sun 9–12, 2–5:30 (Nov–Mar closes at 5). Closed 1 Jan, 1 May, 25 Dec

Few Moderate

Far right: *the medieval Castelvecchio bridge in Verona, city of Romeo and Juliet*

Right: *Treviso, its cobbled streets interspersed with canals, is a little like a smaller, less grand Venice*

28B4

Museo Civico
Borgo Cavour 24
0422 658442
Tue–Sat 9–12,:30, 2:30–5, Sun 9–12. Closed public hols
Cheap

TREVISO

Treviso's walled centre is full of meandering old streets and brooding canals. The medieval and Renaissance buildings of Piazza dei Signori include the church of Santa Lucia, with frescoes by Tommaso da Modena (14th century). Gothic San Nicolò contains more da Modena frescoes on the columns, as well as works by Lorenzo Lotto and others, while the 15th- to 16th-century Duomo has a Titian altarpiece and an 11th-century baptistery. There is good Renaissance art in the **Museo Civico**.

29C4

Castello di San Giusto
Piazza Cattedrale 3
040 313 636
Apr–Sep, 9–7; Oct–Mar, 9–5. Closed public hols
Cheap

TRIESTE

The historic city of Trieste is built on the sea, with most of its hinterland in Slovenia. The city has a long maritime tradition and among its places of interest are the Museo del Mare, which traces the history of seafaring. The early 20th-century Piazza dell'Unita d'Italia opens on to the sea. In the town centre is the fascinating Duomo San Giusto, a 14th-century building linking two 5th-century basilicas that contains spectacular 12th-century mosaics. The splendid 15th- to 16th-century **Castello di San Giusto**, with wonderful views, houses a museum with a good weapons and armour collection.

29C5

Palazzo Arcivescovile
Piazza Patriarcato
0432 25 003
Wed–Sun 10–2, 3:30–6:30
Good
Moderate

UDINE

This pretty, hilly town has excellent views over Friuli towards the Alps from the majestic 16th-century Castello. The Renaissance Piazza della Libertà contains the Porticato di San Giovanni with its clocktower (1527), whose two bronze figures strike a bell on the hour. The nearby Arco Bollani was designed by Palladio (1556). The artist Giambattista Tiepolo (1696–1770) was very active in Udine and his works grace the **Palazzo Arcivescovile** (Archbishop's Palace), the Musei Civici and the 14th-century (much-restored) Duomo.

VERONA ✪✪✪

The Veneto region's second-biggest city after Venice attracts plenty of tourists to its 1st-century BC Roman theatre for outdoor opera in summer (➤ 110). Among Verona's other important monuments is the unusually ornate Romanesque church of **San Zeno Maggiore** (1123–35). Bronze door panels (11th and 12th century) depict scenes from the Bible and the life of San Zeno, while the interior's highlights include a ship's keel ceiling (1376) and an altarpiece by Mantegna (1450s). The two main squares are the elegant Piazza dei Signori, with the 12th-century Palazzo del Comune (town hall) among its medieval and Renaissance civic gems, and the more workaday Piazza delle Erbe, with a busy market. The powerful Scaligeri family, who governed the town from 1260 to 1387, are commemorated by a 14th-century bridge leading to the **Castelvecchio** (with an excellent art collection) and by the Arche Scaligere, their opulent tombs.

28B4

San Zeno Maggiore

Piazza San Zeno

Daily 8:30–12:30, 3–6:30. No admission during services

Castelvecchio

Corso Castelvecchio 2

045 594 734

Tue–Sun 8:30–7:30, Mon 1:30–7:30. Closed public hols

Few

Moderate

VICENZA ✪✪✪

This genteel, gracious city is rich in the works of its most illustrious son, the architect Andrea Palladio (1508–80). Most famous of these is his eye-pleasingly symmetrical villa, **La Rotonda**, which has been copied all over the world. Palladio's first public commission was the graceful double-colonnaded Basilica in Piazza dei Signori, where he also designed the Loggia del Capitaniato. Among the mass of other Palladio buildings are the Teatro Olimpico (1579), the oldest covered theatre in Europe, and many of the *palazzi* on the aptly named Corso Andrea Palladio. The Museo Civico (in another Palladio building) has splendid Gothic and Renaissance art, while older monuments include the Gothic churches of Santa Corona and San Lorenzo and some of the buildings on Contrà Porti, untouched by Palladio.

28B4

Piazza Matteotti 12

0444 320 854; www.ascom.visit

La Rotonda

Via Rotonda 29 (about 2km from Vicenza)

0444 321 793

Gardens: mid-Mar–Oct, Tue–Sun 10–12, 3–6; Interior: Wed only

Moderate

Tuscany & North Central Italy

Populated by the highly cultured Etruscans centuries before the Romans rose to power, this is an area where rural and urban beauty blend harmoniously. While the landscape seems almost to have been sculpted by the Renaissance artists whose works are everywhere, the little hilltowns appear to have grown naturally out of the rock on which they are perched.

Travellers have been flocking to central Italy for centuries to enjoy the way of life that comes with a pleasant climate, excellent food and wines and an unequalled quantity and quality of art and architecture. For many this is quintessential Italy and, although you will have to share its spectacular sights with many others, the quiet confidence that comes from a long and prosperous history imbues even the busiest piazza with a soothing calm and a sense of continuity.

> *'The traveller who has gone to Italy to study the tactile values of Giotto, or the corruption of the papacy, may return remembering nothing but the blue sky and the men and women who live under it.'*
>
> E M FORSTER,
> *A Room with a View*, 1908

Firenze (Florence)

Florence is Renaissance Italy at its civilised best, and can easily claim to have been the heart of the massive artistic movement that swept Europe from the late 13th to the early 16th century. The most accomplished artists and architects of the period flocked to Florence from all over central Italy to work for the powerful families. Today, the compact historic centre of Tuscany's busy capital is a mass of masterpieces from that flourishing era.

Florence's Duomo, with its extravagant façade, was begun in 1296

What to See in Florence

DUOMO AND BATTISTERO (CATHEDRAL AND BAPTISTERY) ✪✪✪

The Duomo's lavish exterior includes Giotto's 85m-high campanile (1334) and illustrative reliefs by Pisano and Lucca della Robbia. The massive dome (1465), by Brunelleschi, was the largest of its time. The façade is 19th century. Inside are intricate marble inlaid floors (16th century), Vasari frescoes in the dome, and works by Lucca della Robbia, Ghiberti, Uccello and others. There's more art in the Museo dell'Opera del Duomo. The nearby octagonal baptistery has splendid carved doors by Ghiberti (north and east) and Pisano (south).

- 59D4
- Piazza del Duomo
- 055 230 2885
- Campanile: 8:30–7; Dome: Mon–Fri 8:30–7, Sat 8:30–4. Closed religious hols; Museo dell'Opera del Duomo: Mon–Sat 9–7:30, Sun 9–2
- 1, 11, 17, 23a
- Few
- Expensive

GALLERIA DELL'ACCADEMIA ✪✪

Modern Europe's first art school, the Accademia delle Belle Arti, was founded here in 1563, and many of its original exhibits were acquired for the students to study and copy. Today the main pull of this collection of 15th- to 19th-century Tuscan art is the Michelangelo sculpture, including the (surprisingly enormous) original of his seductive *David* (1504), created for Piazza della Signoria (➤ 55), where a copy now stands. Among the other outstanding exhibits here are the four bound *Slaves* or *Prisoners* (unfinished, 1521–23) meant for the tomb of Pope Julius II.

- Via Ricasoli 60
- 055 238 8612
- Tue–Sun 8:30–6:20. Closed public hols
- Many routes
- Good
- Expensive

GALLERIA DEGLI UFFIZI (➤ 21, TOP TEN)

Via del Proconsolo 4
055 238 8606
Tue–Sat, 2nd and 4th Sun of month and 1st, 3rd and 5th Mon of month 8:30–1:20. Closed public hols
19
Few (ground floor only)
Moderate

Above: *public executions were once held in the courtyard of the Bargello*

MUSEO NAZIONALE DEL BARGELLO ✪✪✪

This imposing *palazzo* (1255–1345) was the city governor's residence, then from 1574 the police headquarters; public executions were held in its courtyard until 1786. It became one of Italy's first national museums in 1865. What the Uffizi (➤ 21) is to Renaissance painting, the Bargello is to sculpture – many of its exhibits came from the same Medici collections. Michelangelo's works include his first freestanding sculpture, *Bacchus* (1497), while other highlights are Donatello's jaunty *David* (1430), bas-reliefs (1402) by Brunelleschi and Lorenzo Ghiberti, and bronzes by Benvenuto Cellini (1500–71).

Via Cavour 1
055 276 0340
Thu–Tue 9–7. Closed Wed, public hols
1, 6, 7, 11, 12, 14
Few
Moderate
Advance booking recommended

PALAZZO MEDICI-RICCARDI 

Generally acclaimed as the finest example of Florentine Renaissance architecture, the *palazzo* was started in 1444 by Michelozzo for Cosimo Medici the Elder and was the family's home until 1540. Michelangelo may have designed the windows (1517) next to the entrance. In the elegant courtyard are sculptures, and up the right-hand staircase is the Cappella dei Magi with frescoes (1459) by Benozzo Gozzoli.

Piazza de'Pitti
055 238 8614
Palace: Tue–Sun 8:15–6:50; Gardens: Jun–Aug, 8–7:30; Nov–Feb, 8–4:30; Mar and Sep, 8–6:30; Oct 8–5:30 (closed first and last Mon of month). Closed public hols
15, 32, 37, 42
Some access to gardens
Palace expensive, gardens moderate

PALAZZO PITTI AND GIARDINO DI BOBOLI 

Probably designed by Brunelleschi (1458) for the Pitti banking family, this grandiose *palazzo* was their ostentatious attempt to outdo the Medici who, however, were to buy it from the declining Pitti in 1550. It now houses several museums, the most important of which is the Galleria Palatina, where a rich collection of Renaissance masterpieces is hung in frescoed halls. When open, the 17th-century state apartments are well worth seeing, as are the Galleria del Costume's clothes from the 18th to 20th centuries. Next to the *palazzo* are the Boboli Gardens. Laid out for the Medici after 1550, they are a splendid example of 16th- and 17th-century garden design, with much use of water, statues and formal layouts.

PIAZZA DELLA SIGNORIA

The political and social heart of Florence is an outdoor art gallery with Ammanati's Fontana di Nettuno (1575) and a copy of Michelangelo's *David* (now in Galleria dell'Accademia, ➤ 53) among the works that stand outside the Loggia dei Lanzi (1382). In the Loggia are Roman statues, Cellini's *Perseus* (1554) and Giambologna's powerful *Rape of the Sabine Women* (1583), which has a disturbing flaw running down the assailant's marble back. The piazza is dominated by the austere **Palazzo Vecchio** (1332), a monument to civic worthiness puffed out beneath its 94m tower. Its imposing rooms are packed with art by Michelangelo, Vasari, Bronzino, Ghirlandaio and others.

Palazzo Vecchio
- Piazza della Signoria
- 055 276 8465
- Mon–Wed, Fri–Sat 9–7, Sun and Thu 9–2 (summer Mon and Fri 9–11PM). Closed public hols
- 19, 23, 31, 32
- Few
- Moderate

Ponte Vecchio, constantly busy with street traders and pedestrians

PONTE VECCHIO

Florence's oldest and most charming bridge, with little shops and houses clinging precariously to the sides, was designed by Taddeo Gaddi (Giotto's pupil) in 1345.

- Lungarno Archibuscieri
- Many routes

SAN LORENZO

The bare, unfinished façade of this Brunelleschi church (1442–6) hides a Renaissance treasure trove. The bronze pulpits are Donatello's (finished by his pupils in 1460), as are the sacristy decorations and doors (1435–43); the staircase, desks and ceiling of the Biblioteca Medicea Laurenziana are by Michelangelo; and a Bronzino fresco (1659) and some spectacular Medici monuments adorn the main body of the church.

- Piazza di San Lorenzo
- 055 216 634
- Church: Tue–Sat, 2nd and 4th Mon of month 8–5, 1st, 3rd and 5th Sun of month 8–1:50. Closed public hols; Biblioteca: Mon–Sat 8:30–1:30
- Many routes
- Biblioteca: free; Chapel: moderate

SAN MARCO

Founded in the 13th century, the convent of San Marco was extended by Michelozzo in 1437. Some cells are decorated with frescoes by Fra Angelico (1430s and 40s), including a hauntingly lovely *Annunciation*. These form part of the Museo di San Marco, along with a collection of other Renaissance masterpieces.

- Piazza di San Marco
- 055 238 8608
- Mon–Fri 8:15–1:50, Sat, 2nd and 4th Sun of month 8:15–6:50. Closed 1 Jan, 1 May, 25 Dec
- Many routes

SANTA CROCE

Piazza di Santa Croce
055 244 619
Apr–Oct 9–6:30; Nov–Mar 9:30–12:30, 3–6; Sun and hols all year 3–5:30
11, 19, 31, 32

The spacious interior of this Franciscan church (1294 onwards) holds the tombs of Michelangelo (1570, by Vasari), Machiavelli and other Renaissance greats. The artworks are too numerous to mention, but include Luca della Robbia roundels in Brunelleschi's Cappella de'Pazzi, Giotto frescoes in the Cappelle Bardi and Peruzzi, a Donatello wooden crucifix, and frescoes (including an early night scene) by Taddeo Gaddi.

SANTA MARIA DEL CARMINE

Piazza del Carmine
055 238 2195
Mon, Wed–Sat 10–5, Sun 1–5. Closed public hols, 7 Jan and 16 Jul
15

Fortunately the magnificent Cappella Brancaccio frescoes survived a fire which badly damaged the rest of the church in the 18th century. The frescoes, depicting the Life of St Peter, were started by Masolino (1420s) and finished by Filippino Lippi (1480), but the bulk of them are by Masolino's pupil, the Renaissance pioneer Masaccio (1401–28). His realism, expressiveness and use of perspective were carefully studied by subsequent artists. Look out for the anguished *Adam and Eve Being Expelled from Eden* (to the left), and the facial expressions of characters in the other scenes.

SANTA MARIA NOVELLA

Piazza di Santa Maria Novella
055 282 187
Church: Mon–Thu and Sat 9:30–5, Fri and Sun 1–5; Museum: Mon–Thu and Fri–Sat 9–2
Cheap

Three founders of the Renaissance movement are represented in this 13th-century church: Alberti, with his dramatic black-and-white marble façade (1458); Brunelleschi, with his wooden crucifix; and Masaccio, whose use of perspective in the splendid Trinity fresco (1428) was revolutionary for its time. In addition, there are frescoes (1485) by Ghirlandaio in the Cappella Tornabuoni, while the museum housed in the cloisters contains numerous frescoes, including some by Uccello. These were badly damaged in 1966 when the River Arno flooded.

Part of Alberti's façade for Santa Maria Novella

What to See in North Central Italy

ANCONA

The capital of the province of Le Marche (The Marches) was founded on the Adriatic coast in the 4th or 5th century BC. Survivors from its early history include a fine collection of Hellenic, Etruscan and Roman art and artefacts in the **Museo Archeologico Nazionale delle Marche** and the well-preserved Arco di Traiano (Trajan's Arch, AD 115) overlooking the port. Several later historic monuments survived heavy World War II bombing; among these are the 15th-century Loggia dei Mercanti, with a Gothic façade, and 10th-century Santa Maria della Piazza; with floor mosaics from an earlier church on the same site.

29C4

Museo Archeologico Nazionale delle Marche

Palazzo Ferretti, Via Ferretti 6

071 202 602

Tue–Sun 8:30–7:30. Closed 1 Jan, 1 May, 25 Dec

Few

Moderate

AREZZO

Originally a major Etruscan and Roman centre, Arezzo preserves remains from its ancient past in the **Museo Archeologico** overlooking a 1st-century Roman amphitheatre. Since then, this wealthy city's many illustrious sons have included Guido d'Arezzo (the 10th-century inventor of the musical scale), the poet Petrarch (1304–74) and the artist and art historian Giorgio Vasari (1511–74), who built, decorated and lived in **Casa Vasari**. He also contributed to the centuries of work done on **Pieve** (parish church) **di Santa Maria**. Arezzo's main crowd-puller, however, is the church of **San Francesco,** with Piero della Francesca's recently restored, magnificent soft-coloured frescoes (1452–66). These illustrate the incident-packed life story of Christ's cross from its origins in the Garden of Eden to its final rediscovery and rescue by St Helena, mother of the emperor Constantine. The **Museo d'Arte Medievale e Moderna** has a good collection of 14th- to 19th-century Tuscan art.

59E3

Museo Archeologico

Via Margaritone 10

0575 20 882

Daily 8:30–7:30

Few

Moderate

Casa Vasari

Via XX Settembre 55

Pieve di Santa Maria

Corso Italia

San Francesco

Piazza San Francesco

0575 900 404

Mon–Sat 9–6, Sun 1–5:30. Booking essential (06 32 810)

Good

Moderate

Museo d'Arte Medievale e Moderna

Via di San Lorentino 8

0575 409 050

Tue–Sun 9–7. Closed public hols

Moderate

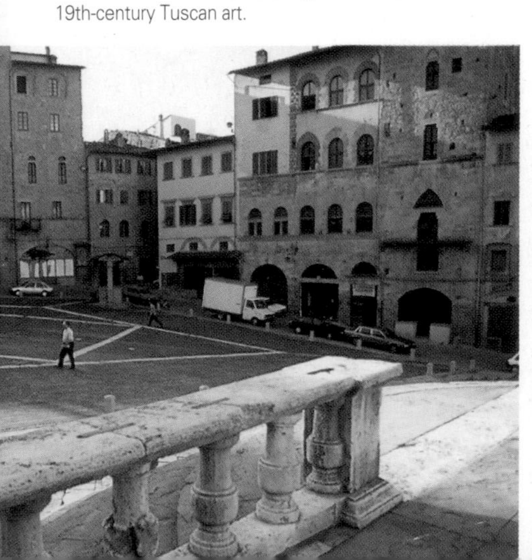

Giorgio Vasari designed the portico on the square of Arezzo's unusually sloping Piazza Grande

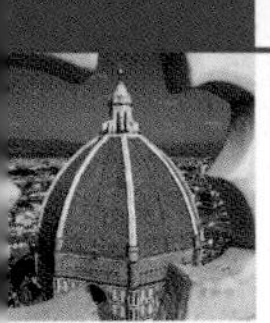

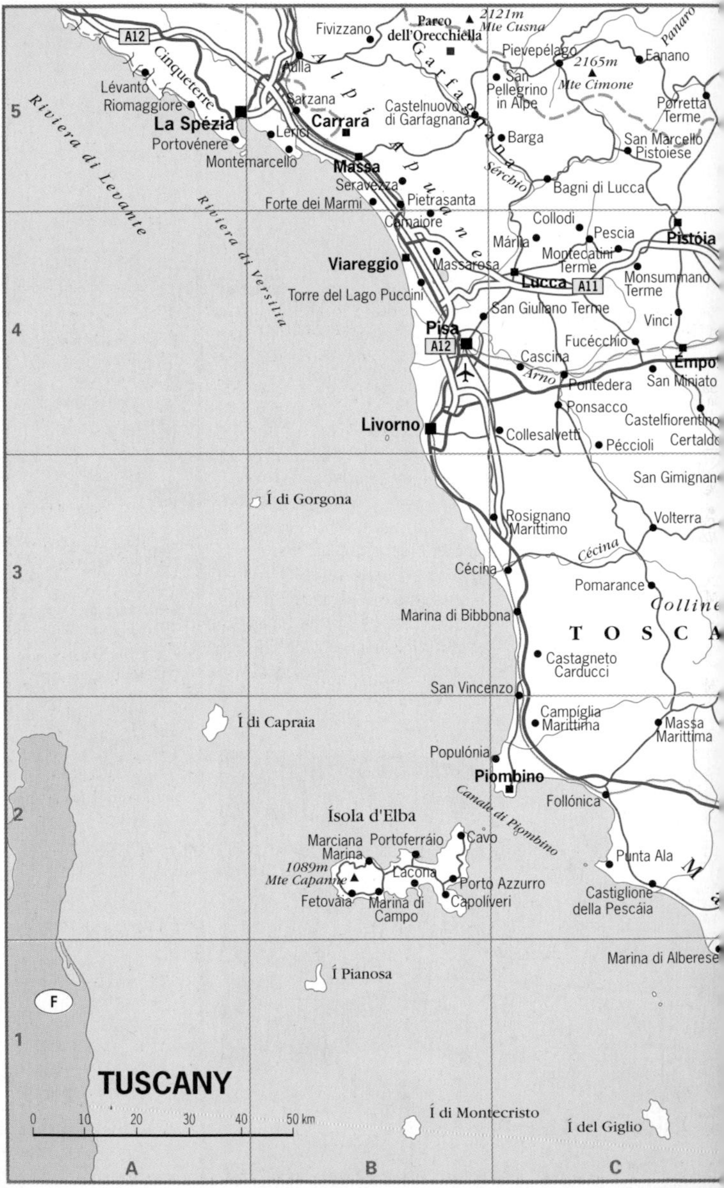
TUSCANY
A12
A11
Cinqueterre
Lévanto
Riomaggiore
La Spézia
Portovénere
Montemarcello
Lerici
Sarzana
Aulla
Fivizzano
Parco dell'Orecchiella
2121m Mte Cusna
Alpi Apuane
Garfagnana
Carrara
Massa
Castelnuovo di Garfagnana
Pievepélago
2165m Mte Cimone
San Pellegrino in Alpe
Fanano
Panaro
Porretta Terme
Barga
San Marcello Pistoiese
Sérchio
Bagni di Lucca
Seravezza
Pietrasanta
Forte dei Marmi
Camaiore
Collodi
Pescia
Pistóia
Márlia
Montecatini Terme
Viareggio
Massarosa
Lucca
Monsummano Terme
Torre del Lago Puccini
San Giuliano Terme
Vinci
Pisa
Fucécchio
Cascina
Arno
Empo
Pontedera
San Miniato
Ponsacco
Livorno
Castelfiorentino
Collesalvetti
Péccioli
Certaldo
San Gimignano
Í di Gorgona
Rosignano Marittimo
Volterra
Cécina
Pomarance
Colline
Marina di Bibbona
TOSCA
Castagneto Carducci
San Vincenzo
Campíglia Marittima
Massa Marittima
Í di Capraia
Populónia
Piombino
Follónica
Canale di Piombino
Ísola d'Elba
Marciana Marina
Portoferráio
Cavo
1089m Mte Capanne
Lacona
Porto Azzurro
Fetovaia
Marina di Campo
Capolíveri
Punta Ala
Castiglione della Pescáia
Marina di Alberese
Í Pianosa
F
Í di Montecristo
Í del Giglio
Riviera di Levante
Riviera di Versilia
0
10
20
30
40
50 km
A
B
C
1
2
3
4
5

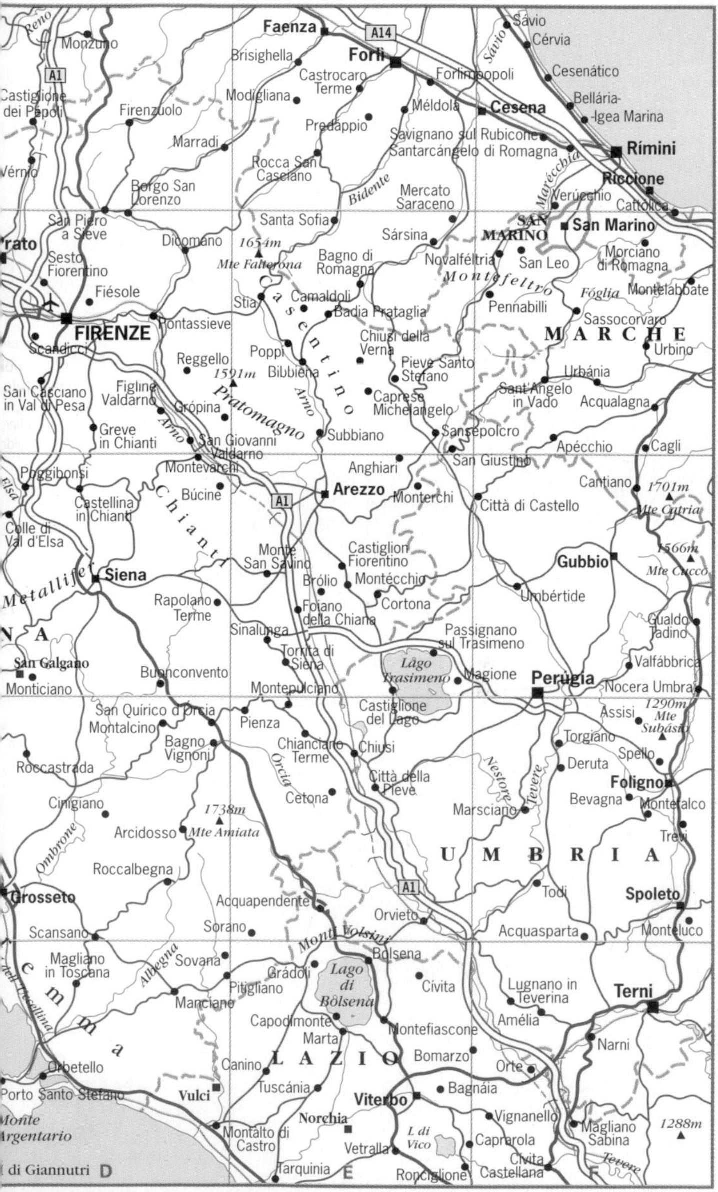

TUSCANY & NORTH CENTRAL ITALY

Reno
Monzuno
Faenza
A14
Sávio
Cérvia
Brisighella
Forlì
A1
Castrocaro Terme
Forlimpopoli
Cesenático
Castiglione dei Pépoli
Modigliana
Méldola
Cesena
Bellária-Igea Marina
Firenzuolo
Predáppio
Savignano sul Rubicone
Marradi
Santarcángelo di Romagna
Rímini
Vérnio
Rocca San Casciano
Marecchia
Riccione
Borgo San Lorenzo
Bidente
Mercato Saraceno
Verúcchio
Cattolica
San Piero a Sieve
Santa Sofia
SAN MARINO
San Marino
Prato
Dicomano
1654m
Sársina
Mte Falterona
Sesto Fiorentino
Bagno di Romagna
Novalféltria
San Leo
Morciano di Romagna
Montefeltro
Fiésole
Camaldoli
Fóglia
Montelabbate
Stia
Casentino
Pennabilli
FIRENZE
Pontassieve
Badia Prataglia
Sassocorvaro
MARCHE
Scandicci
Poppi
Chiusi della Verna
Urbino
Reggello
Pieve Santo Stefano
Urbánia
Bibbiena
1591m
San Casciano in Val di Pesa
Figline Valdarno
Arno
Caprese Michelangelo
Sant'Angelo in Vado
Acqualagna
Grópina
Pratomagno
Greve in Chianti
Subbiano
Sansepolcro
Apécchio
Cagli
San Giovanni Valdarno
San Giustino
Poggibonsi
Montevarchi
Anghiari
Cantiano
Elsa
Búcine
Arezzo
1701m
Chianti
Monterchi
Città di Castello
Mte Catria
Castellina in Chianti
Colle di Val d'Elsa
Castiglion Fiorentino
1566m
Monte San Savino
Gubbio
Mte Cucco
Siena
Brólio
Montécchio
Metallifere
Rapolano Terme
Foiano della Chiana
Cortona
Umbértide
Gualdo Tadino
Sinalunga
Passignano sul Trasimeno
Torrita di Siena
Valfábbrica
San Galgano
Buonconvento
Lago Trasimeno
Magione
Perúgia
Monticiano
Montepulciano
Nocera Umbra
San Quírico d'Órcia
Castiglione del Lago
Assisi
1290m
Mte Subásio
Montalcino
Pienza
Torgiano
Bagno Vignoni
Chianciano Terme
Chiusi
Spello
Roccastrada
Órcia
Deruta
Nestore
Città della Pieve
Foligno
Tevere
Cinigiano
Cetona
Bevagna
Montefalco
1738m
Marsciano
Arcidosso
Mte Amiata
Trevi
Ombrone
UMBRIA
Roccalbegna
Todi
Grosseto
Acquapendente
A1
Spoleto
Orvieto
Sorano
Acquasparta
Scansano
Monti Volsini
Monteluco
Bolsena
Magliano in Toscana
Sovana
Albegna
Grádoli
Lago di Bolsena
Cívita
Lugnano in Teverina
Pitigliano
Terni
Manciano
Amélia
Capodimonte
Montefiascone
Maremma
Marta
Narni
Orbetello
Canino
LAZIO
Bomarzo
Orte
Tuscánia
Bagnáia
Porto Santo Stefano
Vulci
Viterbo
Monte Argentario
Norchia
Vignanello
Magliano Sabina
1288m
Montalto di Castro
L di Vico
Caprarola
Vetralla
Cívita Castellana
Tevere
I di Giannutri
D
Tarquinia
E
Ronciglione
F

29C3

Opposite: *hilltop Cortona has wonderful views of the Tuscan countryside*
Below: *St Francis reputedly preached to animals; Assisi's Rocca Maggiore*

ASCOLI PICENO ✪

The medieval historic centre of this dignified walled town more or less follows the grid street plan of the old Roman Asculum Picenum. At its heart lies Piazza del Popolo, whose highlights are the 13th-century Palazzo dei Capitani del Popolo, with a Renaissance doorway by Cola d'Amatrice, the church of San Francesco (1258–1549), and the adjoining Loggia dei Mercanti (1513) where merchants carried out their business. On stately old Piazza dell'Arringo there is a 12th-century Duomo, with another Amatrice façade, a Carlo Crivelli polyptych (1473) inside and a splendid 12th-century baptistery.

59F2

Basilica di San Francesco
Piazza San Francesco
075 819 001
Mon–Sat 9:30–12, 2:30–6. Closed public hols
Cheap

Duomo
Piazza San Ruffino

Rocca Maggiore
Via Maria delle Rose
Daily 9 to sunset

Santa Chiara
Piazza Santa Chiara

ASSISI ✪✪✪

One of the most visited places in Europe, Assisi was at the heart of a series of earthquakes that shook central Italy in autumn 1997. Many important historic buildings were very badly damaged and among the worst architectural casualties was the **Basilica di San Francesco**, St Francis's burial place and Assisi's most important monument. Started in 1228, this magnificent church contained matchless frescoes by Giotto, Cimabue, Lorenzetti and others. Many of these were virtually destroyed, but have since been magnificently restored. Other monuments include the 12th- and 13th-century Romanesque **Duomo** huddled next to its hefty campanile; the impressively positioned 14th-century castle, **Rocca Maggiore**; and the church of **Santa Chiara**, with Giotto-influenced interior frescoes. Assisi's oldest monument, the 1st-century BC Tempio di Minerva (converted into a church), on the attractive Piazza del Comune, escaped the earthquake unscathed.

CORTONA ✪

This perfect example of a Tuscan hilltown was founded by the Etruscans, whose artefacts, along with other ancient remains, can be seen in the **Museo dell'Accademia Etrusca** within the imposing Palazzo Pretorio, one of the late medieval civic buildings on the beautiful Piazza della Repubblica. The Museo Diocesano, housed in a deconsecrated church, has works by Fra Angelico, Signorelli (who was born in Cortona) and others.

59E3

Museo dell'Accademia Etrusca

Piazza Signorelli 19

0575 637 235

Apr–Sep, Tue–Sun, 10–7; Oct–Mar, Tue–Sun 10–5

Moderate

ELBA ✪

Napoleon was exiled on this lush little island after his 1814 abdication. He led a simple life from his country **Villa San Martino,** but a rash escape attempt led to exile for real on bleak St Helena in the Atlantic Ocean. Apart from enjoying the beautiful bays, cliffs, fishing villages and inland scenery, visitors today can admire the view from 1,000m Monte Capanne and explore the intriguing museums in Portoferraio and Marciano.

28B3

from Piombino

Villa San Martino

San Martino

0565 915 846

Tue–Sat 9–8; Sun, public hols 9–1:30. Closed 1 Jan, 25 Dec

Moderate

GUBBIO ✪✪

Clinging to the lower slopes of Monte Ingino, this enchanting Umbrian town has remained essentially unchanged since the Middle Ages. Along its winding streets of heavy, full-bodied houses are mysterious narrow doorways, evocatively called *porte della morte* (doors of death). The main monuments include the hefty Palazzo dei Consoli (1332), whose Museo Civico has 3rd-century BC Etruscan inscribed tablets; the Palazzo Ducale (1470) with its fine Renaissance courtyard; the Gothic **Duomo**; and the 13th-century church of **San Francesco**, with frescoes (1404–13) by Ottaviano Nelli. The stage-like, elevated Piazza della Signoria (or Piazza Grande) is on a man-made platform.

59F3

Duomo

Via Ducale

San Francesco

Piazza 40 Martiri

Did you know ?

Every year at the end of May, three vast, phallic, wooden 'ceri' (candles), each 4m long, are raced by competing teams through Gubbio and up to the church of Sant'Ubaldo on top of 820m Monte Ingino. You can see them in the church by climbing the mountain or taking the cable-car from Porta Romana.

Lucca

Distance
3km

Time
1 hour without stops; 3–4 hours with stops

Start point
Piazza Napoleone

End point
Piazza San Martino

Lunch
Del Teatro (€€)
Piazza Napoleone 25
0583 493 740
Closed Tue

A rooftop view of Lucca from the tower of Palazzo Guinigi, seat of the medieval lords of Lucca

Surrounded by a wall, with a walkway on the ramparts, this medieval-Renaissance city has retained its original regular street layout from ancient times.

Start at Piazza Napoleone.

The square is dominated by a statue of Napoleon's niece, Marie Louise de Bourbon, and the 16th-century Palazzo della Provincia.

Head north-northeast up Via Vittorio Veneto to San Michele in Foro.

The exuberance of the façade of this 12th- to 14th-century church is juxtaposed with a serene interior.

Rejoin the same road (now called Via Calderia).

On the left (corner of Via di Poggio) is the house where composer Giacomo Puccini was born in 1858.

Go on up Via Calderia, cross Via Buia into Via Cesare Battisti and follow it to San Frediano.

The façade has a vibrant 13th-century mosaic of the Ascension, and inside is a gigantic Romanesque font with carvings of scenes from the Lives of Christ and Moses. Southeast of Piazza San Frediano, across Via Filungo, is the Piazza del Mercato. The square follows the outline of the Roman amphitheatre that stood here.

Head back to the centre on Via Filungo, turn left down Via Sant-Andrea and follow it to the Palazzo dei Guinigi.

The tower of this Gothic, 14th-century red-brick building has trees growing out of its top.

Head south-southwest down Via Sant' Anastasia until you reach the Basilica of San Martino.

This excellent example of 12th- to 14th-century Pisan-Lucchese architecture has an assymetrical façade, squeezed in to make room for the campanile. Inside are exquisite artworks. Opposite the basilica is the ancient church of Santi Giovanni e Reparata, rebuilt in the 17th century; the portal is original 12th century.

MAREMMA ✪

Italy's answer to the Wild West, where *butteri* (cowboys) herd docile horned cattle and stage rodeo shows, lies along the coast of southern Tuscany. Much of this flat, scrubby marshland falls within the **Parco Nazionale dell'Uccellina,** with marked footpaths and picnic areas. Evocative ruined defence towers, built by the Medici in the 16th century, overlook the Maremma's wide, undeveloped beaches. To its north lie salt marshes.

58C2
To Grosseto
To Grosseto

Parco Nazionale dell'Uccellina
Centro Visite di Alberese
0564 407 098
Daily 8:30–sunset

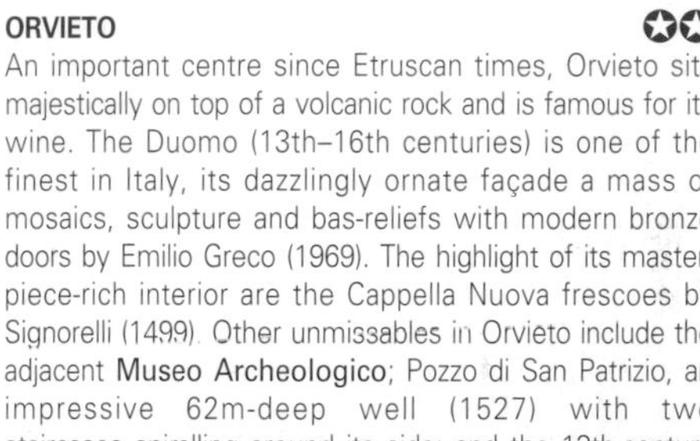

ORVIETO ✪✪

An important centre since Etruscan times, Orvieto sits majestically on top of a volcanic rock and is famous for its wine. The Duomo (13th–16th centuries) is one of the finest in Italy, its dazzlingly ornate façade a mass of mosaics, sculpture and bas-reliefs with modern bronze doors by Emilio Greco (1969). The highlight of its masterpiece-rich interior are the Cappella Nuova frescoes by Signorelli (1499). Other unmissables in Orvieto include the adjacent **Museo Archeologico**; Pozzo di San Patrizio, an impressive 62m-deep well (1527) with two staircases spiralling around its side; and the 13th-century Palazzo del Popolo.

59E2

Museo Archeologico
Piazza Duomo
0763 341 511
Apr–Sep, 9:30–6; Oct–Mar, Tue–Sun 10–5. Closed 1 Jan, 25–26 Dec
Few
Moderate

San Domenico convent in Perugia, home of the Museo Archeologico Nazionale dell'Umbria

PERUGIA ✪✪

The outskirts of the capital of Umbria are a bustling, modern, urban sprawl, but the city centre is pure Renaissance, focused on the dramatic Piazza IV Novembre and its 13th-century Fontana Maggiore. Also on the piazza are the majestic Palazzo dei Priori (13th century), its inner walls frescoed by Cavallini (1273–1308), Perugino (1445–1523) and others, and the fine Gothic Cathedral with a baroque doorway. The **Galleria Nazionale d'Umbria** has the region's best collection of 13th- to 18th-century art. Elsewhere in the city, important monuments include the Museo Archeologico Nazionale dell'Umbria; and the serene Oratorio di San Bernardino (1457–61), with bas-reliefs by Agostino di Duccio.

59F3

Galleria Nazionale d'Umbria
Corso Vannucci
075 574 1257
Daily 8:30–7. Closed 1st Mon of month, public hols
Good
Expensive

58B4

Torre Pendente
Campo dei Miracoli
050 560 547
Expensive
Summer 8–7:20; winter 9–5. Visits every 40 minutes.
Buy tickets in advance from the ticket office at the Towers

PISA

Pisa's most famous landmark, the 54m **Leaning Tower (Torre Pendente)**, was leaning so much (about 5.5m) that it was closed to the public from 1990 until 2001 for major restoration. Built between 1173 and 1350 as the Duomo's campanile, it started to lean in 1274. It is one of four dreamlike monuments on the surreally perfect Campo dei Miracoli (Piazza Duomo). Buscheto started the Duomo in 1064. Inside are a pulpit (1302–11) carved by Pisano and mosaics (1302) by Cimabue. There is another carved pulpit in the Battistero (12th–13th centuries) with Gothic decoration by Pisano. Although the Camposanto cemetery was badly bombed in World War II, traces of its 14th-century frescoes have survived. The Museo Nazionale di San Matteo houses 13th- to 17th-century Tuscan art, notably *Andrea* by Pisano; Piazza dei Cavalieri with many Renaissance buildings by Vasari; and Santa Maria della Spina (1230–1323), a sugary Gothic creation rebuilt on its present site in 1871 to avoid flooding.

58C4

San Giovanni Fuorcivitas
Via Cavour

Ospedale del Ceppo
Piazza Giovanni XXII

Above: *Pisa's tower may one day lean too far*

PISTOIA

The heart of this industrial town's walled historic centre is Piazza del Duomo, with the 14th-century Gothic Battistero and the 12th- to 13th-century Duomo, both in striped dark and light marble. Inside the Duomo is the sumptuous silver altar of St James (1287–1456). Further afield lie the churches of Sant'Andrea (12th century), with pulpit and crucifix (1298–1308) by Pisano, and **San Giovanni Fuorcivitas** (12th–14th centuries), with a Taddeo Gaddi polyptych and a Luca della Robbia terracotta. The **Ospedale del Ceppo** has a unique terracotta frieze by Luca's great-nephew, Giovanni della Robbia.

SAN GALGANO 

The romantic skeleton of a 13th-century abbey, dissolved in the 17th century, lies surrounded by lush trees and fields between Siena and Massa Marittima. It was built by Cistercian monks in French Gothic style, and its soothing, grassy remains give an insight into how such buildings were constructed. Overlooking the abbey is the circular Capella di Montesiepi, containing a sword miraculously thrust into rock by Galgano and frescoes of scenes from the saint's life (1344) by Ambrogio Lorenzetti.

59D3
Bus from Siena

Above: *San Gimignano, a Tuscan tourist honeypot*

SAN GIMIGNANO 

The skyline of San Gimignano, one of the prettiest and most visited medieval hilltowns in Tuscany, is dominated by 13 towers erected by competing noble families in the 12th and 13th centuries. At its heart lie Piazza della Cisterna, with a lovely medieval well, and Piazza del Duomo, where the 12th- to 13th-century **Collegiata** contains magnificent art by Ghirlandaio (1448–94) and others. There is more exceptional early Renaissance art in the Museo Civico, housed in the 13th-century Palazzo del Popolo, whose 54m-high tower is the town's tallest. The 13th-century church of Sant'Agostino has frescoes by Benozzo Gozzoli among its impressive artworks.

58C3
Piazza Duomo 1
0577 940 008

Collegiata
Piazza del Duomo
0577 942 226
Mon–Sat 9:30–7:30, (till 5 Nov–Mar), Sun 1–5
Moderate

SAN MARINO 

The capital of this 60sq km independent republic (which issues its own coins and postage stamps and has its own splendidly uniformed army and police force) is perched on a precipitous cliff, with vertiginous views from the footpath that links its three picture-book **Rocche** (castles); one of them contains a museum of arms. It is a fun place to visit, but its immaculate, over-restored centre, swarming with tourists, has a slightly inauthentic atmosphere.

59F4

Access by bus

Rocche
Jun–Sep 8–8; Oct–May 9–5
Cheap

59D3

Museo Civico

0577 292 226

Mid-Mar to Nov, 10–7; Dec to mid-Mar 10–6:30

Expensive

SIENA ✪✪✪

Winding streets of dignified medieval and Renaissance buildings open out on to the main Piazza del Campo, a dramatic, sloping, theatre-shaped piazza with the 13th- to 14th-century Palazzo Pubblico at its foot. Inside the *palazzo* is the **Museo Civico**, whose frescoes of *Good and Bad Government* (Lorenzetti, 1338–40) symbolise the philosophy of this civilised city. Towering over the *palazzo* is the 102m Torre del Mangia (1138), with excellent views at the top of its 505 stairs. Every summer competing local teams, each wearing different colours, race horses round the piazza in the *Palio* (➤ 116). Behind the opulent façade of the Duomo (1136–1382) lies a wealth of art treasures, including Pinturicchio frescoes (1509) in the Piccolomini Library, a font by della Quercia and Donatello, and a magnificent marble inlaid floor. The Museo dell'Opera del Duomo and the Pinacoteca Nazionale contain other important artworks. Civic relics from Siena's past are on show in the Palazzo Piccolomini (1460s).

Did you know ?

Siena's (and Italy's) patron saint, St Catherine of Siena (1347–80), dedicated herself to God at the age of eight and became a holy mystic. Her house (Via Camporeggio 37) is full of illustrations of her life while her preserved head is in the church of San Domenico (1226 onwards) along with frescoes by the explicitly nicknamed Sodoma and others.

59F2

Arco di Druso

Piazza del Mercato

Duomo

Piazza del Duomo

SPOLETO ✪✪

Famous for its international arts festival (➤ 111), this breathtaking Umbrian town contains relics from a history that dates back to pre-Roman times. These include the 1st-century BC **Arco di Druso** (Arch of Drusus) and the monumental, 80m-high, 230m-long Ponte delle Torri (Bridge of Towers), built in the 12th century over the remains of a Roman aqueduct. The unusually graceful façade of the 12th-century **Duomo** has no fewer than eight rose windows; inside, a 17th-century restoration includes works by Bernini, Pinturicchio and Carracci.

TODI

Spilling over the edge of its hilltop location, this pretty town is notable for its medieval architecture. Piazza del Popolo, at its heart, is the setting for the 13th-century Palazzo del Capitano, Palazzo del Priori and Palazzo del Popolo, housing the restored **Museo Etrusco-Romano and Pinacoteca** (picture gallery). The regal Romanesque-Gothic Duomo contains fine Renaissance stalls, while the church of San Fortunato is a pleasing mix of Gothic and Renaissance with frescoes (1432) by Masolino. One of the best gems of the Italian Renaissance, the church of Santa Maria della Consolazione (probably planned by Bramante), lies on the Orvieto road, on the outskirts of Todi.

59F2

Museo Etrusco-Romano and Pinacoteca

Piazza del Popolo
075 894 4148
Apr–Aug, Tue–Sun 10:30–1, 2:30–6; Oct–Feb, Tue–Sun 10:30–1, 2–4:30; Mar, Sep, Tue–Sun 10:30–1, 2–5. Closed Mon except Apr
Good
Moderate

Opposite: *Siena's Piazza del Campo, one of Italy's great public spaces, hosts the twice-yearly* Palio

Left: *high above the Tiber, Todi has three sets of concentric walls – Etruscan, Roman and medieval*

URBINO

The Renaissance genius Raphael (1483–1520) was born here. One of the few works he left to his home town is in the **Galleria Nazionale delle Marche**, housed in the Renaissance Palazzo Ducale (1444–82), alongside other masterpieces by the likes of Lucca della Robbia, Uccello and Piero della Francesca; Casa di Raffaello contains only copies of Raphael's paintings. The Duomo was rebuilt by Valadier after an earthquake in 1789. The oratories of San Giuseppe (16th century) and San Giovanni Battista (late 14th century) are also worth visiting; the first for its fine crib and the second for frescoes (1416) by brothers Giacomo and Lorenzo Salimbeni.

59F4

Galleria Nazionale delle Marche

Piazza Duca Federico
0722 2760
Mon 8:30–2, Tue–Sun 8:30AM–9:15PM; Jun–Sep, Sat 8:30AM–11AM. Closed 1 Jan, 1 May, 25 Dec
Few
Moderate

VOLTERRA 

This is one of the best places to see Etruscan remains. These include parts of the Arco Etrusco (the rest is Roman) and the unrivalled **Museo Etrusco Guarnacci**'s collection. There is also a fine 1st-century BC Roman theatre. Other sights include excellent 14th- to 17th-century Tuscan art in the Pinacoteca and Museo Civico; austere 13th-century *palazzi* on Piazza dei Priori; and a pleasingly simple Romanesque Duomo, with 13th-century sculpture and baptistery and 12th-century bas-reliefs on the 17th-century pulpit.

58C3

Museo Etrusco Guarnacci

Via Don Minzoni 15
0588 86 347
Mid-Mar to Oct 9–6:45; Nov to mid-Mar 9–1. Closed 1 Jan, 25 Dec
Expensive (includes entrance to Pinacoteca)

Food & Drink

Italians are justly proud of their cuisine, which is among the finest and (according to research) the most healthy in the world. Although certain staples can be found all over the country, each region has its own specialities, based on history, tradition and the best of local produce.

Primi (First Course)

Pasta comes in a wide variety of shapes and with every imaginable accompanying sauce (*condimento*). *Spaghetti alle vongole* (with clams) can be found in most coastal regions. *Pesto* – chopped basil, olive oil, Parmesan cheese and pine nuts – is a Ligurian speciality, while *ragù* (meat sauce) is common in central Italy, *carbonara* (bacon, eggs and pecorino cheese) in Rome, and pasta with sardines in Sicily. Rice is often used in place of pasta, especially in the north near the Po Valley, where it is grown. It is used in dishes such as *risotto alla Milanese* and with black squid ink in Venice (and also Sicily). Polenta is another particularly northern alternative to pasta; a thick, porridge-like or even solid substance made from ground maize.

Highly valued truffles come from Piedmont (the white variety) and Umbria (black variety)

Secondi (Main Course)

Veal (*vitello*) and chicken (*pollo*) are common throughout Italy. Lamb (*agnello*) is more common in south central and southern Italy, while beef (*manzo*) is used in the north. In Abruzzo, goat is a speciality, especially in spring, and wild boar (*cinghale*) appears on many north central menus. Wide use is made in many areas of offal (liver, kidneys, heart and even brains and intestines) and horsemeat (or donkey in Sardinia), famed for its high iron and low fat contents. Fish and seafood include sardines, mussels, clams, tuna and swordfish (the last two particularly in the south), while lakeside areas make good use of fresh-water fish and eels.

Risotto is popular in northern regions where rice is grown

Many varieties of cheese are produced in Italy, some made locally in farms and sold on market stalls

Contorni (Vegetables)

A massive range of mushrooms (including the popular *funghi porcini*) come in particular from central Italy where, together with truffles, they are gathered wild during spring and autumn. Tangy rocket leaves are used in salads and with cold meats, while deep-fried courgette flowers, in batter with a hint of anchovy and cheese, are a common snack and *antipasto* option. The Rome area is famous for artichokes, while the best tomatoes come from Calabria.

Dolci (Desserts)

Apart from the ubiquitous *tiramisù* and *gelati*, you'll be tempted by such delights as *torta a ricotta* in the south and south central regions; *cantucci* (hard almond biscuits) served with sweet *vin santo* for dunking in Tuscany, and light, spongy *panettone*, a Milanese speciality.

Wines and Drinks

Almost anywhere you go in Italy, the basic wines served as house wine in restaurants range from reliably drinkable to good. Top-quality reds come from Piedmont (Barolo, Dolcetto and Barbera d'Alba) and Tuscany (Vino Nobile di Montepulciano, Brunello di Montalcino and Chianti Classico). The best of whites and sparkling wines include still Collio Pinot Bianco and lightly sparkling Prosecco from the northeast, sparkling Moscato d'Asti from the northwest, and still Orvieto Classico from Umbria. Marsala and dessert wines are a particular Sicilian speciality.

The massive list of drinks to stimulate your appetite (*aperitivi*) includes Campari and Martini, while, to help you digest, *digestivi* include *grappas* that range from firewater to silky smooth, and *amari* – thick, sticky concoctions made with herbs.

The quality of Italian wines is guaranteed by the DOC system, similar to the French Appellation Controllé

South Central Italy

This is the area in which the rich, cosmopolitan north meets the more traditional, mellow *mezzogiorno* (south) – not just geographically but culturally and gastronomically as well. The best place to see the resulting blend of cut-and-thrust northern Europe with the slower paced Mediterranean way of life is Rome, where politicians and business people rush through sun-soaked piazzas and strolling crowds. Apart from Rome and its immediate vicinity, south central Italy is slightly off the tourist track and even the beaches, while just as well developed as those elsewhere in Italy, don't attract the same international crowd, catering instead to hordes of weekenders from nearby towns and cities. To the east of Rome lie the rugged mountains of Abruzzo and Molise. Here, age-old isolated communities serve as centres for hillwalking in summer and skiing in winter.

> *'Perhaps the world can hardly offer a more interesting outlook than that from the tower of the Roman Capitol. The eye leaps ... to the mountains.'*
>
> GEORGE ELIOT,
> *Journals from Italy*, 1860

Rome: St Peter's and the Vatican from the Tiber

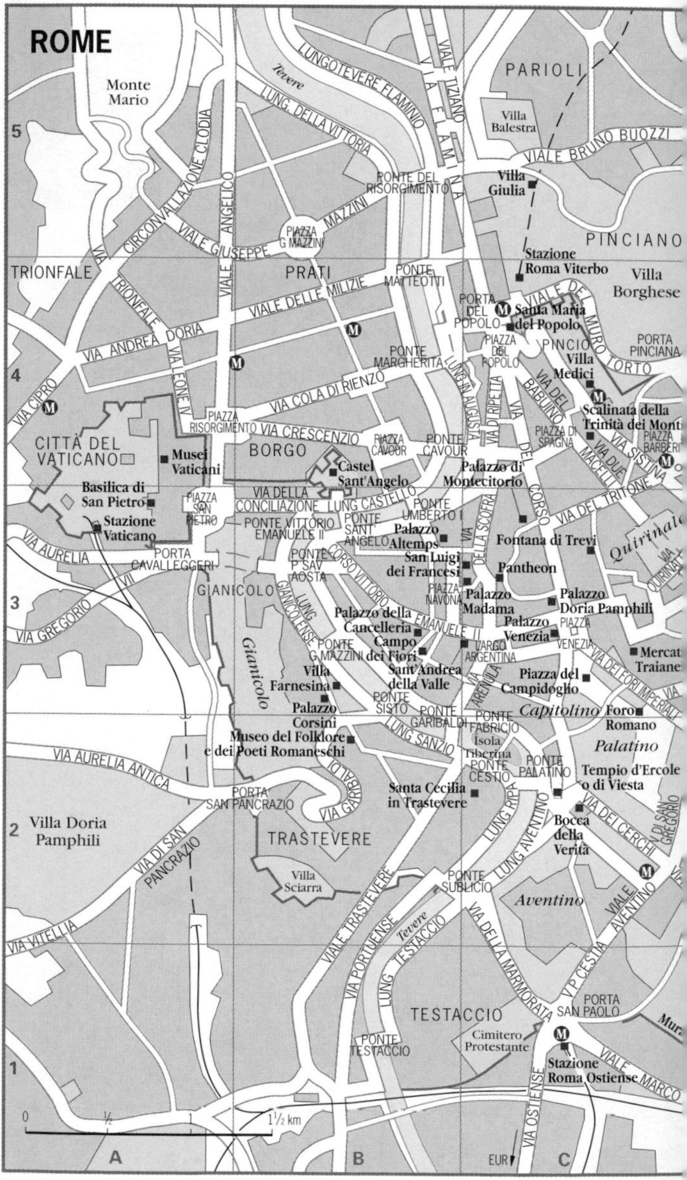

ROME

Monte Mario
Pariolі
Villa Balestra
Villa Giulia
Pinciano
Stazione Roma Viterbo
Villa Borghese
Trionfale
Prati
Porta del Popolo
Santa Maria del Popolo
Piazza del Popolo
Pincio
Villa Medici
Porta Pinciana
Scalinata della Trinità dei Monti
Piazza di Spagna
Piazza Barberini
Città del Vaticano
Musei Vaticani
Borgo
Castel Sant'Angelo
Piazza Cavour
Palazzo di Montecitorio
Basilica di San Pietro
Piazza San Pietro
Stazione Vaticano
Palazzo Altemps
San Luigi dei Francesi
Fontana di Trevi
Quirinale
Pantheon
Piazza Navona
Palazzo Madama
Palazzo Doria Pamphili
Porta Cavalleggeri
Gianicolo
Palazzo della Cancelleria
Campo dei Fiori
Sant'Andrea della Valle
Palazzo Venezia
Piazza Venezia
Mercati Traianei
Largo Argentina
Piazza del Campidoglio
Capitolino
Foro Romano
Villa Farnesina
Palazzo Corsini
Museo del Folklore e dei Poeti Romaneschi
Isola Tiberina
Palatino
Tempio d'Ercole o di Viesta
Santa Cecilia in Trastevere
Porta San Pancrazio
Villa Doria Pamphili
Trastevere
Bocca della Verità
Villa Sciarra
Aventino
Testaccio
Porta San Paolo
Cimitero Protestante
Stazione Roma Ostiense
EUR
Viale Tiziano
Via Flaminia
Lungotevere Flaminio
Lung. della Vittoria
Tevere
Viale Bruno Buozzi
Ponte del Risorgimento
Circonvallazione Clodia
Viale Angelico
Piazza G. Mazzini
Viale Mazzini
Viale Giuseppe Mazzini
Via Trionfale
Ponte Matteotti
Viale del Muro Torto
Viale delle Milizie
Via Andrea Doria
Ponte Margherita
Via Leone IV
Via Cola di Rienzo
Lung. in Augusta
Via di Ripetta
Via del Babuino
Via Cipro
Piazza Risorgimento
Via Crescenzio
Ponte Cavour
Via Sistina
Via Due Macelli
Via della Conciliazione
Lung. Castello
Ponte Umberto I
Via della Scrofa
Via del Corso
Via del Tritone
Ponte Vittorio Emanuele II
Ponte Sant'Angelo
Via Aurelia
Ponte P. Sav. Aosta
Corso Vittorio Emanuele II
Via Quirinale
Via Gregorio VII
Lung. Gianicolense
Ponte G. Mazzini
Via Arenula
Via dei Fori Imperiali
Ponte Sisto
Ponte Garibaldi
Ponte Fabricio
Lung. Sanzio
Via Aurelia Antica
Ponte Cestio
Ponte Palatino
Via Garibaldi
Via di San Gregorio
Via dei Cerchi
Via di San Pancrazio
Lung. Ripa
Lung. Aventino
Ponte Sublicio
Viale Aventino
Via Vitellia
Viale Trastevere
Via Portuense
Lung. Testaccio
Via della Marmorata
V. P. Cestia
Ponte Testaccio
Mura
Viale Marco Polo
Via Ostiense
0 ½ 1 1½ km
1 2 3 4 5
A B C

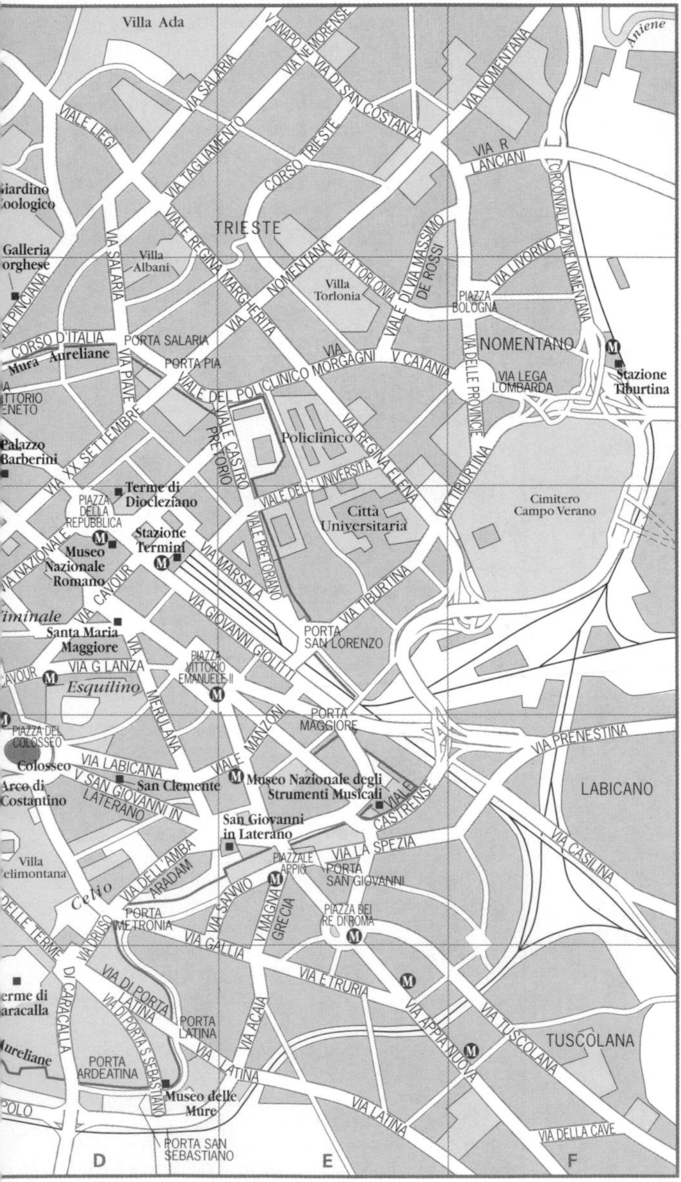

Villa Ada
Aniene
V. ANAPO
VIA NEMORENSE
VIA DI SAN COSTANZA
VIA NOMENTANA
VIA SALARIA
VIALE LIEGI
VIA TAGLIAMENTO
CORSO TRIESTE
VIA R LANCIANI
CIRCONVALLAZIONE NOMENTANA
Giardino Zoologico
TRIESTE
VIALE REGINA MARGHERITA
VIA MASSIMO DE ROSSI
VIALE DI VIA MASSIMO
VIA A TORLONIA
Galleria Borghese
VIA SALARIA
Villa Albani
VIA NOMENTANA
Villa Torlonia
VIA LIVORNO
PIAZZA BOLOGNA
VIA PINCIANA
CORSO D'ITALIA
PORTA SALARIA
Mura Aureliane
VIA PIAVE
PORTA PIA
VIA MORGAGNI
V CATANIA
NOMENTANO
VIA DELLE PROVINCIE
Stazione Tiburtina
VIA LEGA LOMBARDA
VIA VITTORIO VENETO
VIALE DEL POLICLINICO
VIALE CASTRO PRETORIO
Palazzo Barberini
VIA XX SETTEMBRE
Policlinico
VIA REGINA ELENA
VIA TIBURTINA
Terme di Diocleziano
VIALE DELL'UNIVERSITÀ
PIAZZA DELLA REPUBBLICA
Città Universitaria
Cimitero Campo Verano
Stazione Termini
VIALE PRETORIANO
Museo Nazionale Romano
VIA NAZIONALE
VIA CAVOUR
VIA MARSALA
Viminale
VIA TIBURTINA
VIA GIOVANNI GIOLITTI
Santa Maria Maggiore
PORTA SAN LORENZO
PIAZZA VITTORIO EMANUELE II
VIA G LANZA
VIA CAVOUR
Esquilino
VIA MERULANA
PORTA MAGGIORE
VIALE MANZONI
PIAZZA DEL COLOSSEO
VIA PRENESTINA
VIA LABICANA
Colosseo
LABICANO
Arco di Costantino
San Clemente
Museo Nazionale degli Strumenti Musicali
V SAN GIOVANNI IN LATERANO
VIALE CASTRENSE
San Giovanni in Laterano
VIA CASILINA
VIA LA SPEZIA
PIAZZALE APPIO
PORTA SAN GIOVANNI
Villa Celimontana
VIA DELL'AMBA ARADAM
Celio
VIA SANNIO
V MAGNA GRECIA
PIAZZA DEI RE DI ROMA
PORTA METRONIA
VIA DRUSO
VIA GALLIA
DELLE TERME
VIA ETRURIA
Terme di Caracalla
DI CARACALLA
VIA DI PORTA LATINA
VIA DI PORTA S SEBASTIANO
PORTA LATINA
VIA ACAIA
VIA APPIA NUOVA
VIA TUSCOLANA
TUSCOLANA
Aureliane
PORTA ARDEATINA
VIA LATINA
Museo delle Mure
POLO
VIA LATINA
VIA DELLA CAVE
PORTA SAN SEBASTIANO
D
E
F

Bernini's David *in the Galleria Borghese, probably a self-portrait*

Roma (Rome)

Italy's biggest city and capital has well over 2,000 years of history packed into the narrow, winding streets and cramped yet majestic piazzas of its vast historic centre. Its greatest monuments include the civic and religious headquarters of an ancient empire, churches founded during the earliest days of Christianity, and pompous baroque palaces built for the powerful noble families who supplied centuries' worth of scheming popes and amassed vast collections of works by the great artists they patronised.

What to See in Rome

BASILICA SAN PIETRO AND IL VATICANO
(➤ 16–17, TOP TEN)

72C2
Santa Maria in Cosmedin, Via Teatro di Marcello
44, 81, 95, 160, 170, 204

BOCCA DELLA VERITÀ

In the portico of the 12th-century church of Santa Maria in Cosmedin (note the fine inlaid Cosmati marble pavement inside) is a strange, ancient marble face (originally a drain cover) with an open mouth. Legend has it that the mouth will clamp shut on the hand of anybody who lies – during the Middle Ages it was a common test of wives' marital fidelity. Across the road are the rectangular temple of Portunus (2nd century BC) and the round temple of Hercules (1st century BC).

72C3

Museii Capitolini
Piazza del Campidoglio
06 3996 7800
Tue–Sun 9–8
44, 56, 60, 640, 810

Art Centre ACEA
Viale Ostiense 106
06 574 8030
Tue–Sun 9:30–7
Expensive

CAMPIDOGLIO

Michelangelo designed Rome's magnificent civic centre, which today houses the mayor's office in the salmon-pink Palazzo Senatorio and the **Museii Capitolini** in the flanking Palazzi Nuovo and dei Conservatori. The central piazza contains a copy of the 2nd-century AD statue of Marcus Aurelius. In the late 1990s the museums underwent a major revamp and some of the priceless ancient statues were transferred to the incongruous yet atmospheric surroundings of a former electricity power plant near Ostiense station, **the Art Centre ACEA**, where Roman heads, creamy Venuses and other works are exhibited next to obsolete industrial machinery. Highlights from the main museums including the sensual *Dying Gaul*, the delightful 1st-century BC boy extracting a thorn from his foot, and the *She-Wolf Suckling Romulus and Remus* (the symbol of Rome) will return to their natural habitat. The picture gallery has works by Caravaggio, Guercino, Pietro da Cortona, Guido Reni, Tintoretto and others.

CASTEL SANT'ANGELO ✪✪✪

Built by Emperor Hadrian (117–138) as a mausoleum for himself, the *castel* was used as a defensive stronghold by generations of popes from the Middle Ages until the unification of Italy. Since 1886 it has been open to the public, who enter via the original ramp used by Hadrian's funeral procession. Other highlights include a courtyard with Montelupo's statue of an angel (1544) sheathing a sword, and a Michelangelo façade (1514). Off the courtyard are the delicately frescoed (mid-16th century) state rooms including the Sala di Apollo, where holes in the floor lead to notorious prisons, and the magnificent Sala Paolina, with a delightfully enigmatic *trompe l'oeil* door. There are good views over Rome from the ramparts.

- 72B4
- Lungotevere Castello 50
- 06 681 9111
- 87, 280, 492
- Tue–Sun 9–8
- Moderate

The Castel Sant'Angelo is approached by a bridge adorned with Bernini's angels over the Tiber

FORO ROMANO, PALATINO AND COLOSSEO
(➤ 20, TOP TEN)

GALLERIA BORGHESE ✪✪✪

The sculpture, on the ground floor, includes important classical works (*Sleeping Hermaphrodite*, *Dancing Faun*) and Canova's famous sculpture of Napoleon's sister, Pauline Bonaparte Borghese, as a seductive Venus. The highlights, however, are the spectacular early sculptures by Bernini, showing his precocious talent in works such as *The Rape of Proserpine*. Among the celebrated paintings on the ground-floor walls and upstairs are a *Deposition* by Raphael; Titian's early masterpiece, *Sacred and Profane Love*; a rich, vibrant *Last Supper* by Jacopo Bassano; and Correggio's erotic *Danaë*. The six Caravaggio paintings include his important early work, the luscious *Boy with a Fruit Basket*.

- 73D4
- Piazzale Scipione Borghese 5, Villa Borghese
- 06 328 101
- 52, 53, 116, 910
- Tue–Sat 9–7; Booking compulsory
- Expensive

PALAZZO ALTEMPS 

- 72B3
- Piazza San Apollinare 44
- 06 3996 7700
- 70, 81, 87, 115, 116, 186, 492, 628
- Tue–Sun 9–7:45
- Few
- Moderate

This lovingly restored baroque *palazzo* is the perfect setting for the vast ancient sculpture collection amassed in the 16th century by Prince Ludovisi. The prince hired some of the best sculptors of his own time (including Bernini and Algardi) to patch up damaged specimens among his newly acquired Greek and Roman masterpieces. Some of the results are ridiculous, with spare heads and limbs spliced on to unmatching torsos. However, even the most demanding ancient-art purists should find something here that doesn't make them laugh.

PALAZZO BARBERINI 

- 73D4
- Via Quattro Fontane 13
- 06 32810
- 60, 61, 62, 175, 492, 590
- Tue–Sun 9–7
- Moderate
- Booking private apartments in advance

A national art gallery since 1949, this is one of Rome's grandest baroque palaces – Carlo Maderno, Bernini and Borromini all worked on its exterior, while its sumptuous interior includes an elaborate ceiling fresco by Pietro da Cortona in the *Gran Salone*. The collection gives a good overview of (principally Italian) 13th- to 17th-century painting but excels in its 16th- and 17th-century paintings by the likes of Andrea del Sarto, Raphael, Bernini, El Greco, Bronzino, Guido Reni, Guercino and Caravaggio.

Palazzo Doria Pamphili

PALAZZO DORIA PAMPHILI 

- 72C3
- Piazza del Collegio Romano 1a
- 06 679 7323
- Fri–Wed 10–5. Closed Thu, public hols and 15 Aug. State rooms closed for restoration.

This has been the seat of the noble Roman family of Doria Pamphili since the late Renaissance. In the grand reception rooms and picture galleries, with their elaborate frescoed ceilings, the paintings are hung exactly as they were in the 18th century, cluttered side by side from floor to ceiling. They include works by Memling, Raphael, Titian, Tintoretto and Caravaggio. The star of the collection is Velasquez's portrait of Pope Innocent X, resplendent in vermilion robes.

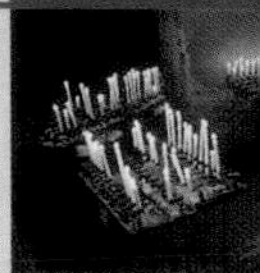

Rome's Historic Centre

Combine this walk with visits to the Forum (➤ 20) and St Peter's and the Vatican (➤ 16–17) and you can claim to have 'done' Rome.

From Largo Argentina follow Corso Vittorio Emanuele to Via Paradiso (left) and head into the pretty market place, Campo de'Fiori.

From here enter Piazza della Cancelleria, where Palazzo della Cancelleria (1485–1513) contains papal offices.

Turn right on Corso Vittorio Emanuele; cross at the lights at Museo Baracco (ancient sculpture). Continue down Via Cuccagna into Piazza Navona (➤ 78). Halfway up the piazza, Corsa Agone leads right to Palazzo Madama.

This 16th-century palace is now the seat of the Senate. Via Salvatore runs alongside it to San Luigi dei Francesi (left), containing Caravaggio paintings.

Continue straight to the Pantheon (➤ 78). Turn right opposite the Pantheon into Vicolo della Madalene, right down Via del Vicario into Piazza del Montecitorio (Parliament House). Follow Via di Guglia, in front of the palazzo, *turning left at Via dei Pastini into Piazza di Pietra (columns of a 2nd-century AD temple of Hadrian). Go down Via di Pietra, cross Via del Corso and continue up Via di Muratte.*

You come to the famous Trevi fountain (1762 by Nicola Salvi); throw in a coin if you want to return to Rome.

Follow Via della Stamperia, turn right up Via del Tritone, cross and turn left on Via Due Macelli to Piazza di Spagna.

Pause on the Spanish Steps before climbing them and turning left, past 16th-century Villa Medici.

Take the path on the right to the Pincio (great views). Continue down into Piazza del Popolo.

Santa Maria del Popolo church contains Caravaggio works.

Distance
4½km

Time
1½ hours without stops,
3–4 hours with stops

Start point
Largo Argentina
72C3

End point
Piazza del Popolo
72C4
Flaminio

Lunch
Hostaria Romanesca (€)
Campo de'Fiori 40

The spectacular Trevi fountain: the name derives from 'tre vie', after the three streets that meet here

72C3
Piazza della Rotonda
06 6830 0230
Mon–Sat 8:30–6, Sun 9–6
Good

PANTHEON 

Erected by Emperor Hadrian (1st century AD), this awe-inspiring temple to all the gods became a Christian church in 609 and contains the tombs of Raphael and Vittorio Emanuele, the first king of united Italy. It is a miracle of ancient engineering: the massive semicircular dome, 43.3m in diameter, was constructed by pouring concrete over a wooden framework. The huge bronze doors are ancient Roman, the ornate marble floor is a 19th-century reconstruction of the original, and the subtly vibrant colours of its interior have been restored.

72B3
70, 81, 87, 115, 116, 186, 492, 628

PIAZZA NAVONA 

One of the world's most beautiful squares owes its elongated shape to the 1st-century AD stadium over which it was built (remains lie to its north). The piazza's centre-piece is Bernini's spectacular *Fontana dei Fiumi* (1651), featuring symbolic representations of the rivers Ganges, Danube, Plate and Nile clinging to a massive artificial cliff-face, in front of the church of Sant'Agnese in Agone (the work of, among others, Bernini's great rival Borromini). The figure at the centre of the fountain to the southeast is also by Bernini.

Piazza Navona, with its three splendid fountains and many cafés, is a popular meeting place

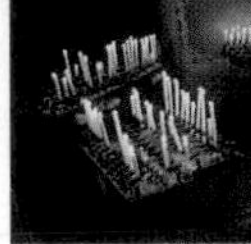

Did you know ?

Benito Mussolini ordered the destruction of many old apartment blocks so that he could construct Via Forii Imperiali, a wide avenue that was ideal for military parades which he could survey from the balcony of Palazzo Venezia.

PIAZZA VENEZIA ✪✪

The hub of central Rome is dominated by the grotesque, white marble monument to Vittorio Emanuele II. To its left is the Renaissance **Palazzo Venezia**, now a museum of applied arts. To its right are the remains of the Mercati Traianei (Trajan's Markets), a 2nd-century AD five-storey shopping mall, which stands behind the intricately carved Trajan's column and the Imperial Forums. They were built by the emperors when the Roman Forum (➤ 20) could no longer handle the business of running Rome.

72C3

Palazzo Venezia

Via del Plebiscito 118

06 679 8865

Tue–Sun 8:30–7

Few

Moderate

SAN CLEMENTE ✪✪

A tour of this three-layered building starts with a 12th-century church containing a lovingly detailed contemporary apse mosaic, a 6th-century choir stall and Masolini frescoes of St Catherine of Alexandria. Beneath this is a 4th-century church containing 11th-century frescoes of St Clement and a large circular well, probably a font. Below this are ancient Roman remains, including a cramped Mithraeum (temple of Mithras) containing a small altar with a relief of Mithras slaying a bull. The route back up passes through the walls of ancient Roman apartment blocks.

74D2

Via San Giovanni in Laterano

06 7045 1018

85, 167, 850

Daily 9–12:30, 3–6

Cheap; Upper church free

SAN GIOVANNI IN LATERANO ✪✪

This was the home of the papacy from the 4th to the 14th centuries, and is now the Cathedral of Rome (the pope doubles up as Bishop of Rome). The building is 16th century with a portico (1585) by Fontana, façade by Galilei and nave (1650) by Borromini. Inside are remnants of earlier buildings, including the bronze door (1190) of the Cappella di San Giovanni Battista and 5th-century mosaics in the exquisite baptistery.

74E2

Piazza San Giovanni in Laterano

06 7720 7991

Basilica: 7AM–7:30PM, Baptistery: 9–1; Cloisters: 9–6

30b, 81, 85, 87, 186, 590, 850

SANTA MARIA MAGGIORE ✪✪

This hefty edifice has a ceiling clad in some of the first gold to be brought back from the New World. The Cappelle Sistina (1585) and Paolina (1611) contain important artworks, but the basilica's main glory lies in its mosaics. On the nave is a 5th-century narrative of the Old Testament and, in the apse, an impressive *Glorification of Mary* (1295). The site of the church is said to have been decided by the Virgin sending an unseasonal fall of snow to this spot, an event still commemorated every August.

74D3

Piazza di Santa Maria Maggiore

Summer 7–7; winter 9–5

16, 70, 71, 75, 84

What to See in South Central Italy

28B3

Villa Aldobrandini
Piazzale Marconi, Frascati
06 942 0331
Mon–Fri 9–1, 3–6 (5 in winter)

Castel Gandolfo
Piazza Plebiscito
Pope gives blessing in courtyard Jun–Sep, Sun noon

CASTELLI ROMANI

The small medieval towns on the slopes of the Alban Hills are close enough to Rome to be reachable for lunch – or even dinner if you have a car and want to enjoy the lights of the city from afar. The white wines they produce are often served as *vino di casa* in Rome's restaurants and *trattorie*. Frascati, the nearest of the Castelli, is dominated by **Villa Aldobrandini** (1598–1603), while Rocca di Papa is the highest (680m) and has fine medieval buildings; the main piazza of Ariccia is adorned by Bernini, and Albano Laziale has Etruscan and Roman ruins. The pope's summer residence is at **Castel Gandolfo**.

59E1

Museo Nazionale di Tarquinia
Piazza Cavour
0766 856 036
Tue–Sun 8:30–7:30. Closed public hols
Moderate (includes visit to necropolis)

ETRURIA

The region of Lazio settled by the Etruscans includes Tarquinia, 2km southeast of which are magnificent painted tombs in the Necropoli di Monterozzi. Tarquinia also has a well-stocked **Museo Nazionale**. Another major Etruscan centre is Cerveteri, where one of the highlights of the Necropoli di Banditaccia (2km north) is the Tomb of the Reliefs, showing scenes from everyday Etruscan life. Vulci, Norchia and Tuscania also have Etruscan remains.

29C3

Museo Nazionale d'Abruzzo
Castello Cinquecentesco
0862 6331
Tue–Sun 9AM–8PM. Closed public hols
Few
Moderate

L'AQUILA

Gran Sasso (2,914m), the highest of the Apennines, towers above the capital of Abruzzo and can best be seen from the majestic 16th-century Castello, which now houses the **Museo Nazionale d'Abruzzo** with its fine collection of art from ancient to modern times. The symbolic Fontana delle 99 Cannelle (Fountain of the 99 Spouts, 1272, but much restored since) has a spout for each of the communities involved in the city's founding in 1240. Other prime monuments are the churches of Santa Maria di Collemaggio (started 1287), with its pink and white geometric façade (14th century), and San Bernardino (1454–72), whose 17th-century restoration includes a baroque ceiling.

The portal of San Silvestre in L'Aquila which is named after the eagle in the imperial arms

OSTIA ANTICA ✪✪

Although nothing like as complete as Pompei (➤ 24), this ancient Roman port (now a long way from the sea) has some fine remains dating from the 1st century BC to the 4th century AD. These stand in a pretty area of encroaching vegetation that creates a park-like atmosphere. Highlights include the mosaics of the Piazzale delle Corporazioni, representing the trading interests of the corporations whose offices stood here; the thermopolium, where hot food and drinks were served (note the illustrated, frescoed menu); the nearby Casa di Diana apartment block; the Terme di Nettuno baths; and a theatre.

- 28B3
- Via Ostiense, Ostia Antica
- 06 565 0022
- Apr–Sep, Tue–Sun 9–7:30; Oct–Mar 9–5
- Metro from Rome
- Moderate

Above: *the Abruzzo National Park is based around a former royal hunting lodge*

PARCO NAZIONALE DI ABRUZZO (ABRUZZO NATIONAL PARK) ✪✪

These 40,000 hectares of mountain wilderness are covered with dense beech and maple forests and shelter many wild animals, including about 100 Marsican brown bears, Apennine wolves, golden eagles, Abruzzi chamois and wild cats. (If you don't manage to spot these in the wild, you can go to the zoo near the park's headquarters to see convalescing injured animals.) The park is well laid out with waymarked trails, picnic areas and campsites.

- 29C3
- Headquarters: Via Consultore 1, Pescasseroli
- 0863 91 955
- Bus from Avezzano or Alfedena

TIVOLI ✪✪

Most people come to this hillside town to see the unusual, spectacular terraced gardens of the **Villa d'Este** (1550), where the statuary, including a row of grotesque heads spitting water, outdoes the plant life. Near by are the stately remains of Villa Adriana. Built for Emperor Hadrian in 118–134, this is an enormous area of ruined follies, including a massive fishpond, the circular Teatro Marittimo on an island in an artificial lake, and many nymphaeums. There are also temples, barracks and a museum.

- 29B3
- Bus from Rome

Villa d'Este

- Piazza Trento, Tivoli
- 0774 312 070

- Tue–Sun 9 to one hour before sunset
- Expensive

South Italy, Sardinia & Sicily

The summer sun rules supreme in the *mezzogiorno* (the south), giving everything an added intensity: colours are brighter, sounds are louder, and flavours richer and more pungent. With the exception of Naples, the Costiera Amalfitana and parts of Sardinia and Sicily, this region is off the international tourist track, so there is plenty to discover. The landscape varies from hostile mountains in Basilicata to flat, fertile plains in Puglia and explosively photogenic coasts in Campania and Calabria. In addition, both the mainland and the islands of Sardinia and Sicily are full of reminders of a long history and centuries of foreign occupation from all corners of Europe and the Mediterranean. South Italy is dotted with prehistoric, Greek and Roman ruins, Norman, Byzantine and Romanesque cathedrals, and effervescent baroque *palazzi* of a lighter, less pompous style than that of their contemporaries to the north.

'The sun is warm, the sky is clear,
The waves are dancing fast and bright,
Blue isles and snowy mountains wear
The purple noon's transparent
might...'

PERCY BYSSHE SHELLEY,
Stanzas Written in Dejection,
Near Naples, 1819

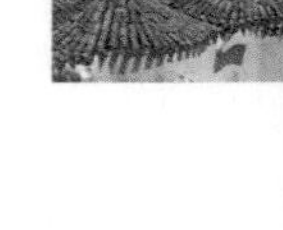

Napoli (Naples)

You either love Naples or hate it; no visitor remains indifferent. This chaotic city and its exuberant inhabitants living on the coast beneath Vesuvius have a character all of their own. In the 18th and 19th centuries, Naples was one of the main stops on the Grand Tour, but during the 20th century crumbling architecture and a soaring crime rate sent the city into decline. A major clean-up programme has greatly improved the situation, but it's still worth taking particular care of your valuables here.

What to See in Naples

CASTEL NUOVO AND PALAZZO REALE

This pleasing caricature of a castle, with crenellations and stolid chess-piece towers, was rebuilt in the 15th century over a 12th-century original. Its majestic entrance is based on ancient Roman triumphal arches. Inside is the 14th-century Cappella Palatina (from the previous building), the Museo Civico and 14th- to 18th-century art. Nearby Palazzo Reale (started by Domenico Fontana in 1600 and heavily restored from the mid-18th century onwards) was the Bourbon royal residence from 1734 to 1860. It contains antique furniture, a library of historic manuscripts, and Neapolitan frescoes (17th–18th centuries).

29C2

Castel Nuovo

Piazza Municipio
081 795 2003
Mon–Sat 9–7
Few
Moderate

Palazzo Reale

Piazza Plebiscito
Thu–Mon 9–8. Closed early Mar, public hols
Moderate

CERTOSA DI SAN MARTINO AND CASTEL SAN ELMO

On a hill with fine views over Naples' historic centre and the bay, this gem of Neapolitan baroque has aristocratic cloisters by Cosimo Fanzago, an opulent, marble-inlaid church and a fascinating museum of traditional Christmas cribs, maps, art, and artefacts illustrating the history of Naples. Behind it stands the star-shaped Castel San Elmo (14th century, rebuilt in the 16th), used as a prison in the 18th century and during the Risorgimento (19th century).

Largo di San Martino
081 578 1769
Tue–Sun 9–7:30
Few
Moderate

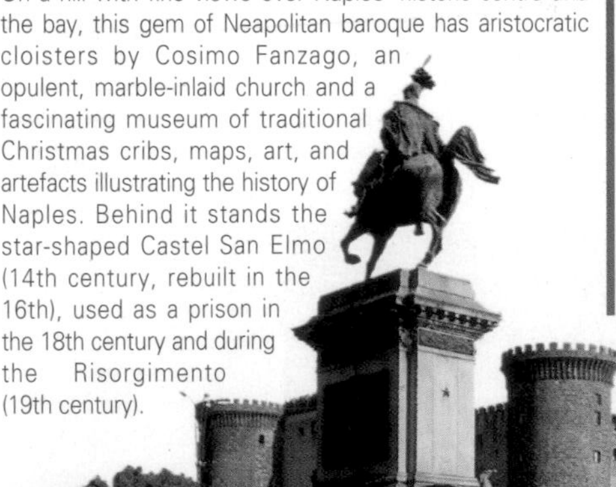

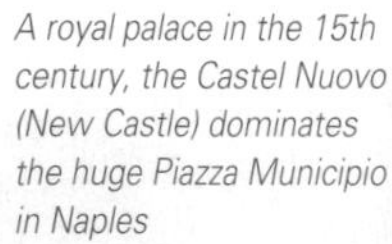

A royal palace in the 15th century, the Castel Nuovo (New Castle) dominates the huge Piazza Municipio in Naples

MUSEO ARCHEOLOGICO NAZIONALE ✪✪✪

- Piazza Museo Nazionale 19
- 081 440 166
- Wed–Mon 9–7. Closed public hols
- Good
- Expensive

If nothing else brings you to Naples, come for this stupendous mass of ancient Greek and Roman artefacts, one of the best such collections in the world. Among treasures too numerous to list are the largest surviving ancient group sculpture (*Amphion and Zethus Tying Dirce to the Horns of the Bull*, 200 BC, from the extensive Farnese collection); some of the most beautiful frescoes, mosaics and other artworks from Pompei (► 24) and Herculaneum (► 86); portrait busts of great Greeks and Romans; and rooms dedicated to erotic art.

MUSEO DI CAPODIMONTE ✪✪✪

- Parco di Capodimonte
- 081 744 1307
- Tue–Sun 9–7:30
- Expensive

Naples' most important art gallery is housed in an 18th-century royal hunting lodge. This is one of the best collections in Italy, with Renaissance and baroque masterpieces (by Masaccio, Bernini, Correggio, Titian, Pieter Brueghel and others), and an interesting section with 19th-century Neapolitan painting.

QUARTIERI SPAGNOLI ✪✪

- West of Via Toledo

This grid of narrow streets below the Certosa di San Martino (► 83) was laid out by Spanish troops in the 17th century and is now a busy, inner-city residential area full of bustle, noise and airing laundry – quintessential Naples as seen in the movies.

SAN LORENZO MAGGIORE AND SAN GREGORIO ARMENO 

San Lorenzo Maggiore
- Via Tribunali 316

San Gregorio Armeno
- Via San Gregorio Armeno 1

Behind an 18th-century baroque façade lies the cool, simple Gothic interior of San Lorenzo Maggiore (14th century) whose tall, slender apse leads the eye automatically upwards. The Gothic mosaic-decorated tomb of Catherine of Austria (died 1323) is here. San Gregorio Armeno, around the corner, is a different story with its over-the-top baroque voluptuousness, which includes frescoes by Luca Giordano. The Benedictine convent attached to the church was a favourite among those daughters of the Neapolitan aristocracy who wished (or were forced) to take the veil.

Below: *a bustling street in the Spanish Quarter – the 'real' Naples*

Did you know ?

San Nicola (Saint Nicholas, or Santa Claus), the patron saint of children, was an Asian bishop who earned his sainthood by (among other equally worthy miracles) resurrecting three children who had been murdered by a butcher, chopped up and preserved in brine. The saint's relics are buried in the crypt of Bari's Basilica di San Nicola.

San Nicola, Bari – an early example of Apulian-Romanesque style

What to See in South Italy

ALBEROBELLO

This strange little town makes the most of its role as the capital of *trulli* country. *Trulli* are the small white buildings with uncemented grey, conical stone roofs that have punctuated the landscape of central Puglia for centuries (although most of the ones you see today are at most 200 years old). As well as its streets of *trulli* homes (many of whose owners are only too happy to give you a guided tour), Alberobello boasts the *trullo* church of Sant'Antonio and the unique two-storied Trullo Sovrano.

29D2

BARI

The capital of Puglia has a labyrinthine historic centre in which the most impressive sights are the imposing **Castello** (1233), whose interesting interior contains casts of other Pugliese monuments, and the Basilica di San Nicola (1087), the first Norman church in the region and much copied elsewhere. The basilica's treasures include a fine 11th-century bishop's throne. One of the buildings based on San Nicola was Bari's Romanesque cathedral (12th–13th centuries), whose interior remains essentially medieval behind a baroque façade.

29D3

Castello
Piazza Federico II di Svevia
Tue–Sun 8:30–7
Cheap

BRINDISI

An important port since Roman times, this slightly drab city today swarms with backpackers and tourists on their way to the many Greece-bound ferries. The Roman column near the port marked the end of Via Appia, which has its beginning in Rome. Brindisi is not the most beautiful city in Italy, but its historic centre does have a certain run-down charm, and there are some good ancient vases in the **Museo Archeologico** opposite the Duomo.

29D2

Museo Archeologico
Piazza Duomo
080 482 7895
Daily 8:30–6:30
Cheap

Houses survived up to two storeys at Herculaneum, buried by mud when Vesuvius erupted in AD 79

29C2
Ferry from Naples, boats from Sorrento and other towns on the Costiera Amalfitana (➤ 18)

Grotta Azzurra
Boat from Marina Grande in Capri harbour (not in rough weather)
Expensive

CAPRI ✪✪

During the day, this beautiful island turns into an anthill of activity as daytrippers are shunted around in a continuous stream of minibuses taking in sights that include the sculpted Faraglioni rocks off the northeast coast, the soothing Certosa di San Giacomo (14th century) in Capri town, and the cable-car from Anacapri to the island's highest point. The highlight, however, is the famous Grotta Azzurra (Blue Grotto) where little boats, packed like sardine tins, whoosh through a low opening into the extraordinary sea-filled hollow in the cliff-face.

29C3
Località Andria, Bari
Mar–Sep, 2:30–7:30; Oct–Feb closes at 6:30
Cheap
Few

CASTEL DEL MONTE ✪✪

From the outside, this octagonal building with a tower on each of its corners resembles a massive sculpture. It was commissioned by Emperor Frederick II in 1240 and is the most attractive and elaborate of the 200 fortresses he had built on his return from the Crusades; he probably used this one as a hunting lodge. Inside, some of its plain, serene vaulted rooms are lined with marble, and there are wonderful views from the ramparts.

COSTIERA AMALFITANA (➤ 18, TOP TEN)

29C2

COSTIERA CALABRESE (CALABRIAN COAST) ✪

The rugged coast of Calabria has some of the cleanest water and most enticing beaches in Italy. Towns such as Scilla, Tropea, Maratea, Palmi and Pizzo are good centres from where to enjoy these, although a car is useful if you want to reach the quietest ones.

29C2
Corso Ercolano, Ercolano
081 739 0963
8:30–7:30 (8:30–5 winter)
Expensive

ERCOLANO (HERCULANEUM) ✪✪

The ancient city of Herculaneum (founded by the ancient Greeks) was buried by mud during the same eruption of Vesuvius that killed off Pompei (➤ 24). The excavations, while not as extensive as Pompei's, include some fine houses with mosaics, baths and a theatre.

Above; the Gargano Peninsula is the spur of Italy's boot, thrusting out into the Adriatic Sea

GARGANO ✪✪

To the northeast of the singularly unprepossessing agricultural town of Foggia is the vibrantly beautiful Gargano promontory, 10,000 hectares of which is covered with the dense beech, pine and maple trees of the Foresta Umbra. Unspoilt white beaches and bays of turquoise water line its coast. The most scenic stretch of road is the one between Mattinata and the resort of Vieste, which has a 13th-century cathedral and from where boats leave to the equally undeveloped Isole Tremiti.

29C3
Bus to Manfredonià, Vieste, Mattinata, Pèschici and Rodi

LECCE (► 22, TOP TEN)

MATERA ✪✪

A handsome Puglian-Romanesque 13th-century **Duomo** stands at the top of this Basilicata city, but it is the strange lower town, the *sassi* district, that is the most fascinating part. This consists of buildings, including churches and a few *palazzi*, scooped out of the rock and closed off with normal façades. The cave-dwelling habit was probably started by 8th-century monks and continued well into the 20th century, although by then many *sassi* had become uninhabitable and their occupants were rehoused. Major restorations are under way to revive this eerie ghost town.

29D2

Duomo
Piazza del Duomo

PAESTUM ✪

The 6th-century BC Greek city of Poseidonia was taken over by the Romans in 273 BC and continued to be occupied until malaria and the threat of Saracen attack led to its abandonment in the 9th century AD. Excavations, started in the 18th century and among the most important in Italy, include the temples of Neptune (5th century BC), Hera and Ceres (both 6th century BC), a stretch of city wall and a Roman forum. The museum has fine bas-reliefs among the other art and artefacts found on the site.

29C2

Zona Archeologica, Paestum
0828 811 016
9 to two hours before sunset. Museum: 8:45–7. Closed 1st and 3rd Mon of month, public hols
Few
Moderate

POMPEI (► 24, TOP TEN)

Coastal Salentino to Taranto

Distance
*c*180km

Time
Half a day without stops; at least a day with stops. Suggestion: take a day to get to Taranto, spending the night there and visiting the Taranto sights the next day.

Start point
Otranto
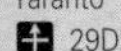 29D2

End point
Taranto
 29D2

Lunch
La Puritate (€)
Via Sant Elia 18, Gallipoli
0833 264 205
Closed Wed, mid-Oct to mid-Nov

The heel of Italy is a region of intensely coloured, pine-lined coasts, cliffs, caves and sparkling white towns.

Start from Otranto.

This walled historic centre has a castle and 12th-century mosaics in the Romanesque Duomo.

Take statale 173 south to the thermal spa of Santa Cesarea and the nearby Grotte Romanelli and Zinzulusa (stalactites, stalagmites and prehistoric finds) and on to Castro.

Castro has a cathedral, 16th-century walls and a port.

Continue south to Marina di Leuca.

The church of Santa Maria di Leuca marks *finibus terrae* – land's end – the southern tip of the peninsula.

Follow the coast through Torre San Giovanni and Marina di Mancaversa to the medieval town of Gallipoli (castle and Duomo), and on to Santa Maria al Bagno, where you head inland to baroque Galatone, then detour to Galatina.

Mending nets in the port of Gallipoli on the Salentine coast, still an important fishing centre

In this wine-making centre, look out for the Lecce baroque architecture and 14th-century Santa Caterina di Alessandra, with frescoes.

Double back to Galatone, taking the road to Nardò (an important centre in the 17th century) and on to Porto Cesareo, to join statale 174 to Manduria, with its Duomo and medieval ghetto, and then Taranto.

Here the atmospherically run-down Città Vecchia (old town) contains a Duomo (with features from the 11th century onwards), a castle and a busy fish market. In the new town, the Museo Archeologico Nazionale is one of the best places to see the exquisite art and artefacts of Magna Graecia (the ancient Greek colonies in southern Italy). Exhibits include sculptures and a massive collection of Greek terracottas.

REGGIO CALABRIA ✪

The main reason for venturing as far as this modern city in the toe of Italy (essentially rebuilt after an earthquake in 1908) is the **Museo Nazionale**, whose prime exhibits are two restored 5th-century BC Greek bronze statues of warriors, fished out of the sea in 1972. Highlights of the upstairs gallery include two 15th-century panel paintings by Antonello da Messina.

29C1

Museo Nazionale

Piazza de Nava 26

0965 812 255

Daily 9–8. Closed 1st and 3rd Mon of month and public hols

Moderate

SARDEGNA (SARDINIA) ✪✪✪

Sardinia's Costa Smeralda (Emerald Coast) has some of the most fashionable beach resorts in Europe, but, if you avoid the glitzy jetset Porto Cervo, you don't have to be a millionaire to enjoy the limpid, turquoise waters that lap this fascinating island's shores. Among its many natural wonders are caves (especially the Grotta di Nettuno), the rugged islands of the Arcipelago della Maddalena, the barren, wild Monti del Gennargentu (rising to 1,800m), and the precipitous road between Arbatax and Dorgali.

Sardinia also has some of the oldest monuments in Europe: the unique *nuraghi* are conical buildings – of uncertain use – made out of blocks of stone and dating back as far as 1500 BC. The best places for seeing *nuraghi* are Dorgali and Barumini. The island of Sant'Antioco has remains of the Phoenician and Roman settlement of Sulcis, and there are more Phoenician traces at Tharros. Remains from prehistoric and ancient Sardinia are in the **Museo Nazionale Archeologico** in Cagliari the enlarged island capital. The cathedral here has splendid 12th-century pulpits, carved by Guglielmo of Pisa with illustrations from the life of Christ. Sassari has the Museo Nazionale Sanna, another fine archaeological collection.

29A2

Ferry from mainland to Cagliari, Olbia and Porto Torres

Airports at Cagliari, Olbia and Alghero

Museo Nazionale Archeologico

Cittadella dei Musei, Piazza Arsenale, Cagliari

070 655 911

Tue–Sun 9–8

Few

Moderate

The beautiful beaches of Sardinia's Emerald Coast are not solely for the rich

29C1

Ferry from Naples or Genoa to Palermo or from Reggio di Calabria to Messina

International flights to Palermo or Catania

Palermo: Piazza Castelnuovo 34 ☎ 091 583 847; Via Cavour 1, Piazza Armerina ☎ 0935 680 201 Siracusa: Via S Sebastiano 43 and 47 ☎ 0931 67 710. Taormina: Piazza S Caterina ☎ 0942 23 243

SICILIA (SICILY)

With a history during which Greek, Phoenician, Roman, Tunisian, Norman, French and Spanish occupations have all left their mark, Sicily has a culture and atmosphere that are subtly different from those of *il continente*, as mainland Italy is called here.

The melancholy city of **Palermo** is the capital. Its historic centre of crumbling baroque *palazzi* contains the Palazzo dei Normanni (Palace of the Normans) and the Cappella Palatina (Palatine Chapel), both with extraordinary Arab-Norman mosaics (12th century); the cathedral (12th to early 19th centuries); and the magnificent churches of La Martorana (Byzantine mosaics), San Giovanni degli Eremiti (Arab influenced) and San Cataldo (12th century). The Galleria Regionale della Sicilia has a major collection of Sicilian art, and the macabre Catacombe dei Cappuccini (Catacombs of the Capuchinas) displays the clothed, mummified remains of 17th- to 19th-century Palermitani.

Near Palermo, the magnificently positioned Duomo at Monreale contains some of the most spectacular 12th- to 13th-century mosaics in existence. Segesta, to the west, has a splendid 5th-century BC temple and a 3rd-century BC theatre. East of Palermo, the pretty fishing village of Cefalù has a Norman cathedral (1131–1240), with more mosaics, and southeast of here, in the middle of Sicily, is Piazza Armerina, where well-preserved mosaics in the Roman villa (3rd–4th century AD) include representations of scantily clad female athletes. **Siracusa** (Syracuse) has a spectacular archaeological area, spanning many centuries of the town's development, a medieval-baroque centre and the Museo Archeologico Regionale. **Taormina**, in a beautiful setting with views of Mount Etna, has another ancient Greek theatre. See also Valle dei Templi (➤ 26).

Above: *pretty Taormina, with fine beaches and thrilling views of Mount Etna, is Sicily's main tourist centre*

Where To...

Above: *wooden Pinochios on a Collodi street stall*
Right: *flower seller in Spello*

The Northwest

Prices
Approximate prices for a three-course meal for one without drinks or service (though a half litre of house wine will often not make much difference to the bill, especially in cheaper places):
€ = up to €20
€€ = €20–35
€€€= more than €35
The bill will usually include a small cover charge (about €1–2 per person) and some restaurants add service (10 to 15 per cent); otherwise tipping is usually about 10 per cent.

Aosta
Ristorante da Nando (€)
Family-run restaurant since 1957. A good selection of *primi* from all over north Italy is followed by game dishes.
Via de Tillier 41 0165 44 455 Lunch, dinner. Closed Mon

Cinqueterre
A Cantina de Mananan (€€)
Good use is made of local fish, salamis and herbs accompanied by wines of the Cinqueterre.
Via Fieschi 117, Vernazza 0187 821 166 Lunch, dinner. Closed Tue, lunch Jun–Sep

Cremona
Porta Mosa (€€)
The *padrone* of this simple *osteria* will help you choose which wines to drink with his lovingly prepared local food.
Via Santa Maria in Betlem 11 0372 411 803 Lunch, dinner. Closed Sun, Aug and 26 Dec–6 Jan

Genoa
Gran Gotto (€€€)
Highly regarded restaurant serving Ligurian specialities, with a particular emphasis on fish.
Viale Brigate Bisagno 69r 010 564 344 Lunch, dinner. Closed Sat lunch, Sun, two weeks in Aug

Lago Maggiore
Osteria dell'Angolo (€€)
Overlooking the lakeside promenade, eat freshwater fish and other local specialities washed down with excellent local wines.
Piazza Garibaldi 35, Verbania 0323 556 362 Lunch, dinner. Closed Nov, Tue and Wed in Dec

Mantua
Due Cavallini (€)
The place to taste hearty Mantuan specialities, including horsemeat, salami, rabbit and pheasant. Not a good choice for those on a diet, or vegetarians.
Via Salnitro 5 0376 322 084 Lunch, dinner. Closed Tue, 20 Jul–20 Aug

Milan
Savini (€€)
The most famous restaurant in Milan, where the glitterati gather on the opening night of the opera season.
Galleria Vittorio Emanuele 02 7200 3433 Lunch, dinner. Closed Sun, New Year and Aug

Trattoria Milanese (€€)
Since 1913 the Valle family have been offering local specialities, including *risotto alla milanese,* in their atmospheric *trattoria.*
Via Santa Marta 11 02 8645 1991 Lunch, dinner. Closed Tue, Jul–end Aug

Pavia
Antica Osteria del Previ (€€)
It's worth travelling out of central Pavia to taste traditional Pavesi fare such as risotto, and *rane fritte* (fried frogs).
Via Milazzo 65 0382 26 203 Lunch (not summer) and dinner. Closed early Jan and Aug

Turin
L'Osto del Borgh Vej (€€)
In the old, medieval quarter near the Duomo; innovative dishes are based on regional favourites with some lighter, modern touches.
Via Torquato Tasso 7 011 436 4843 Lunch, dinner. Closed Sun, Jul or Aug

The Northeast

Bologna

La Farfalla (€)

Excellent-value by Bolognese standards in former red-light district.

Via Bertiera 12 051 225 6560 Lunch, dinner. Closed Sat dinner (in summer), Sun, two weeks Aug, Christmas

Gianni à la Vècia Bulàgna (€€)

Excellent service in welcoming surroundings where the menu includes *bollito* (boiled meat) and *tortellini in brodo,* among other local dishes.

Via Clavature 18 051 229 434 Lunch, dinner. Closed Mon, Sun dinner in summer and all of Aug

Dolomites

Vögele (€€)

Upstairs, an elegant no-smoking restaurant serves refined (and more expensive) versions of the wide range of Alto Adige dishes offered in the less formal downstairs *osteria.*

Via Goethe 3, Bolzano 0471 973 938 Lunch, dinner. Closed Sat dinner, Sun, public hols, two weeks Jul

Ferrara

Antica Trattoria Volano (€)

Local culinary masterpieces in one of Ferrara's oldest *trattorie* (18th century). Not for weight-watchers, although the summer menu is lighter.

Via Volano 0532 761 421 Lunch, dinner. Closed Fri

Modena

Stallo del Pomodoro (€€)

Excellent local cuisine including fine *antipasti* (starters), accompanied by a choice of 200 wines.

Largo Hannover 63 059 214 664 Lunch, dinner. Closed Sat lunch, Sun and Christmas–5 Jan

Padua

L'Anfora (€)

A massive range of dishes for all palates and appetites (including vegetarian), accompanied by a vast selection of wines, in a sociable atmosphere. Open all afternoon.

Via dei Soncin 13 049 656 629 Lunch, dinner. Closed Sun, Aug

Parma

Trattoria dei Corrieri (€€)

Attractively old-style surroundings and a menu that includes a good range of Parma ham, salami and excellent *parmigiano* cheese.

Via Conservatorio 1 0521 234 426 Lunch, dinner. Closed Sun dinner

Ravenna

Ca' de' Vén (€)

Wood-clad wine-bar which has particularly good regional soups washed down with a good local *San Giovese.* Friendly atmosphere.

Via Ricci 24 0544 30 163 Lunch, dinner (open early for both). Closed Mon, Christmas to mid-Jan, one month in summer

Rimini

Osteria de Borg (€€)

Cappelletti in brodo is among the best of a range of fresh pasta dishes followed by simply prepared meats. Good *menu degustazione* (➤ 95).

Via Forzieri 12 0541 56 074 Dinner only (lunch on Sun and hols). Closed Mon, 15–30 Jan

Opening and Closing

In general, restaurants are open for lunch from about 12 until 2:30 and from about 8 to 11 for dinner. Most remain closed one day a week and many are closed for two or more weeks in July or August and/or in November, over Christmas or in January. Most are closed on Christmas Day, 1 May and other public holidays.

What to Eat
A full Italian lunch or dinner starts with *antipasti* (raw and cooked vegetables, cold meats, seafood) followed by the *primo* (first) course of pasta, rice, polenta or soup. *Secondi* are the main courses of meat, fish or cooked cheese accompanied, or followed, by *contorni* (vegetables and salad). The meal finishes with *dolce* (dessert), fruit or cheese and coffee with *digestif* (liqueurs or spirits). Although you don't have to eat your way through all of these, most restaurants expect you to have at least a couple of courses.

Trento

Al Vo' (€€)
A historic *osteria* that claims to date back to the 14th century. The menu concentrates on local food, especially cheeses, meats and salami, which can also be bought to take away
✉ Vicolo del Vo' 11 ☎ 0461 985 374 🕑 Lunch (dinner Thu and Fri only). Closed Sun and late Jun

Treviso

Toni del Spin (€)
The day's specials, which are usually listed on a blackboard, may include (according to the season) soups, tripe and pheasant. There is also a good-value wine list.
✉ Via Inferiore 7 ☎ 0422 543 829 🕑 Lunch, dinner. Closed Sun, Mon lunch, Aug

Trieste

Buffet da Siora Rosa (€–€€)
This is a family-run, traditional, all-day Trieste buffet, with a wide range of substantial local dishes kept hot for instant eating. There is also a restaurant attached if you want to eat at a more leisurely pace.
✉ Piazza Hortis 3 ☎ 040 301 460 🕑 8–8. Closed Sat, Sun, mid-Sep to mid-Oct

Udine

Alla Colonna (€)
A traditional *osteria*, where you can savour the customary *tajut*, a pre-dinner class of wine with your starters. The excellent standard is maintained all the way through to a delicious strudel for dessert.
✉ Via Gemona ☎ 0432 510 177 🕑 Lunch, dinner. Closed Mon lunch, Sun

Venice

Al Mascaron (€€€)
A bustling *trattoria* where booking is recommended; even then you may have to wait to sample a wide choice of authentic Venetian food.
✉ Castello 5525, Calle Lunga Santa Maria Formosa ☎ 041 522 5995 🕑 Lunch, dinner (open early for both). Closed Sun, mid-Dec to mid-Jan

Alle Testiere (€€)
Book to eat local fish-based *primi* and *secondi* in this tiny *trattoria* with a small but well-chosen wine list.
✉ Castello 5801, Calle del Mondo Nuovo ☎ 041 522 7220 🕑 Lunch, dinner. Closed Sun, Mon, Aug, three weeks in winter

Bentigodi da Andrea (€€)
Traditional *osteria* with excellent local soups, fish and meat dishes. Rich desserts are a speciality.
✉ Calesele Cannareggio 1423 ☎ 041 716 269 🕑 Lunch, dinner. Closed Sun

Verona

Al Calmiere (€€)
Well-run restaurant offering the best of simple, satisfying Verona cuisine. Outside eating in summer over-looking the busy piazza.
✉ Piazza San Zeno 10 ☎ 045 803 0765 🕑 Lunch, dinner. Closed Wed dinner, Thu, 1st two weeks Jan

Vicenza

Cinzia e Valerio (€€)
Reservations recommended at this popular restaurant serving the best of Venetian cuisine, especially seafood.
✉ Piazzetta Porta Padova 65 ☎ 0444 505 213 🕑 Lunch, dinner. Closed Sun dinner, Mon, Aug, Christmas–New Year

North Central Italy

Ancona

Gino (€€)

Excellent value for good fresh fish dishes in this pleasant restaurant attached to a hotel near the station.

✉ Piazza Roselli 26
☎ 071 43 310 ⌚ Lunch, dinner. Closed Sun, 23–31 Dec

Arezzo

La Torre di Gnicche (€)

In a 14th-century *palazzo*, a lovingly selected wine list accompanies simple Tuscan soups and *secondi*.

✉ Piaggia San Martino 8
☎ 0575 352 035 ⌚ Dinner only. Closed Wed, Jan

Ascoli Piceno

C'era una volta (€)

Excellent views accompany the good, simple, traditional Marche food and wine; just outside Ascoli Piceno.

✉ Via Piagge 336, Piagge
☎ 0736 261 780 ⌚ Lunch, dinner. Closed Tue

Assisi

Piazzetta dell'Erba (€)

Eat as much as you like in this rustic *osteria* in the medieval heart of Assisi.

✉ Via San Gabriele dell'Addolorata 15
☎ 075 815 352 ⌚ Lunch, dinner. Closed Mon, 10–30 Jan

Cortona

Osteria del Teatro (€€)

A wide range of dishes includes ravioli with courgette flowers and wild boar with polenta.

✉ Via Maffei 5
☎ 0575 630 556 ⌚ Lunch, dinner. Closed Wed, 15–30 Nov

Florence

Acquacotta (€€)

Acquacotta, a local soup made with bread and mushrooms, is among the traditional and innovative dishes served in this quintessential *trattoria*.

✉ Via dei Pilastri 51
☎ 055 242 907 ⌚ Lunch, dinner. Closed Sun, Aug

Al Tranvai (€)

Unpretentious, crowded little *trattoria* in a market square near Santa Maria del Carmine. The menu changes daily to offer the best simple, seasonal dishes.

✉ Piazza Torquato Tasso 14
☎ 055 225 197 ⌚ Lunch, dinner. Closed Sat, Sun, Aug

Gubbio

Federico da Montefeltro (€€)

Eat outdoors at this big restaurant in the historic heart of Gubbio, where Umbrian specialities include truffles.

✉ Via della Repubblica 35
☎ 075 927 3949 ⌚ Lunch, dinner. Closed Thu (not Aug, Sep), Feb

Orvieto

I Sette Consoli (€€)

Excellent service and cooking in elegant surroundings. You can each in the garden in summer. Good *menu degustazione* (➤ panel).

✉ Piazza Sant'Angelo 1
☎ 0763 343 911 ⌚ Lunch, dinner. Closed Sun dinner (Nov–Mar), Wed and part of Feb

Perugia

Aladino (€€)

Family-run restaurant and wine bar where excellent Umbrian dishes are joined by some from Sardinia (the owner is Sardinian).

✉ Via della Prome 11
☎ 075 572 0938 ⌚ Dinner only. Closed Mon, Aug

Tourist Menu versus *Menu Degustazione*

While 'tourist menus' should be treated with caution (Italians have a pretty low opinion of foreigners' gastronomic sensibilities and sometimes seem to think that tourists won't notice if they are served poor-quality food), a *menu degustazione* ('tasting menu') tends to be the sign of a seriously good eating establishment. It usually consists of small portions of several dishes, accompanied by appropriate wines, and is an excellent way of sampling more local specialities than you could normally manage to eat and drink your way through at one sitting.

Snacks and Light Lunches
If you don't want a full meal, most bars have a good range of sandwiches and some have a *tavola calda* (buffet) of hot dishes cooked in advance. *Enoteche* (wine bars) offer plates of cheese, cold meat and other light dishes, while *pizza taglia* sell slices of pizza and a selection of other typically Italian fast food. Finally, *alimentari* (grocers) will fill rolls with whatever they have in stock.

Pisa

La Grotta (€€)
Both menu and wine list change constantly, making the most of what's on offer. Particularly good meat *secondi*, *antipasti* and *primi*, and the desserts are also excellent.
✉ Via San Francesco 103
☎ 050 578 105 Lunch, dinner. Closed Sun, Aug, Christmas–New Year

Pistoia

Lo Storno (€)
This 600-year-old *osteria* offers simple, no-frills Tuscan *primi* and *secondi* washed down with house wine.
✉ Via del Lastrone 8
☎ 0573 26 193 Mon–Wed lunch only, Thu–Sat lunch, dinner. Closed Sun, Aug

San Gimignano

Osteria delle Catene (€€)
Authentic, good-value establishment (rare in a town overrun by tourists). The good local wine list features resinous Vernaccia di San Gimignano among the whites.
✉ Via Mainardi 18
☎ 0577 941 966 Lunch, dinner. Closed Wed, Jan

San Marino

La Fratta (€€)
Classical cuisine (grilled meats a speciality) served here, where outdoor tables nestle under the Rocca.
✉ Salita alla Rocca 14
☎ 0549 991 594 Lunch, dinner. Closed Wed in winter, Mon dinner and Jan–Feb

Siena

Castelvecchio (€)
Adventurous menu mixes Tuscan specialities with dishes from all over Italy and abroad. Good range of vegetable-based *secondi;* fine wines from Tuscany and other Italian regions.
✉ Via Castelvecchio 65
☎ 0577 49 586 Lunch, dinner. Closed Tue

Sportellino (€€)
Delicious local favourites make use of seasonal produce such as salamis, game, mushrooms and chestnuts. Wine from the restaurant's own vineyard.
✉ Via Cerquiglia 4
☎ 0743 45 230 Lunch, dinner. Closed Thu, Jul

Todi

La Mulinella (€)
Just outside Todi, with good views from its garden; unpretentious local dishes have been enthusiastically prepared by chef Irma Pericolini for over 30 years.
✉ Ponte Naia 29
☎ 075 894 4779 Lunch, dinner. Closed Wed, Nov

Urbino

il Cortegiano (€€€)
Central Italian cuisine (including truffles) in this comfortable restaurant, with outdoor dining in summer.
✉ Via Puccinotti 13
☎ 0722 320 307 Lunch, dinner. Closed mid-Dec to Jan

Volterra

Trattoria del Sacco Fiorentino (€€)
Beyond the *trattoria*, which serves innovative dishes based on regional specialities, is a wine bar offering delicious *primi* and simple *secondi*.
✉ Piazza XX Settembre 18
☎ 0588 88 537 ☎ Lunch, dinner. Closed Wed and part of Jan and Feb

South Central Italy

Abruzzo National Park

Plistia (€€)
Abruzzesi cuisine at its very best in this attractive, well-run restaurant attached to a hotel. *Menu degustazione* (➤ 95) with eight courses.
Via Principe di Napoli 28, Pescasseroli ☎ 0863 910 732 Lunch, dinner. Closed Mon

L'Aquila

Trattoria del Giaguaro (€€)
Robust Abruzzi fare that includes *macaroni alla chitarra* and filling meat dishes.
Piazza Santa Maria Paganica 4 ☎ 0862 28 249 Lunch, dinner. Closed Mon dinner, Tue, two weeks in Jul and Aug, Christmas

Castelli Romani

Zarazà (€€)
Summer dining on the terrace overlooking the lights of Rome. Famous for its Lazio cuisine.
Via Regina Margherita 45, Frascati ☎ 06 942 2053 Lunch, dinner. Closed Mon and part of Aug

Ostia Antica

Il Monumento (€€)
Simple, well-made fish dishes at this *trattoria* in the village near the excavations. *Spaghetti monumento* contains a mix of seafood.
Piazza Umberto I 18 ☎ 06 565 0021 Lunch, dinner. Closed Mon

Rome

Il Convivio (€€€)
Creative cuisine served with a touch of genius; good set menus and extensive wine list for special occasions.
Vicolo dei Soldati 31 ☎ 06 686 9432 Lunch, dinner. Closed Sun, Aug

Da Gino (€)
Politicians and journalists jostle for a seat in this popular city eatery to enjoy homemade pasta and each day's traditional dish: gnocchi and *ossobuco* (Thu), *baccalà* (Fri), tripe (Sat).
Vicolo Rosini 4 ☎ 06 687 3434 Lunch, dinner. Closed Sun, Aug

Ditirambo (€€)
This restaurant specialises in innovative Italian dishes based on traditional ingredients in subtle combinations. Homemade bread and pasta; excellent house wine.
Piazza della Cancelleria 74 ☎ 06 687 1626 Lunch, dinner. Closed Mon, Aug

Pizzeria San Calisto (€)
Vast, thin-based pizzas topped with tasty, fresh ingredients in the bustling Trastevere district. Outdoor eating in summer.
Piazza San Calisto 9 ☎ 06 581 8256 Lunch, dinner. Closed Mon

Silvio all'Suburra (€€)
Simple, exquisitely prepared traditional Roman dishes which make the most of seasonal produce.
Via Urbana 67 ☎ 06 486 531 Lunch, dinner. Closed Mon

Tivoli

Villa Esedra (€)
Near the remains of Villa Adriana, with outside eating in summer; innovative *antipasti* and *primi* followed by good, standard *secondi* and desserts.
Via di Villa Adriana 51 ☎ 0774 534 716 Lunch, dinner. Closed Mon

Pizzas
The best pizzas have a hint of charcoal around the edges. This is because they are cooked in a wood oven (*forno a legna*), which creates a temperature that seems unbearable in summer. Not all pizzas are the same; Roman ones have a thin, crisp base, while in Naples pizzas come on a thick, bread-like base, which is more filling. *Calzoni*, a particularly appetite-satisfying option, are made from folded-over pizza dough stuffed with the filling of your choice.

The South

Vegetarians
There are very few vegetarian restaurants *per se* in Italy, and purely vegetarian dishes are seldom marked on the menu. However, wherever you are, even if you don't eat any animal products at all it should be easy to find a good range of pasta dishes including no fish, meat, eggs or cheese; you can follow this with a selection of vegetable *contorni* and grilled cheese (if you eat it). The Italian for vegetarian is *vegetarianio/a*.

Alberobello

La Cantina (€)
Friendly, family-run *trattoria* in the heart of the capital of Trulli country, with a menu that changes seasonally according to the best local ingredients that are available.
✉ Vicolo F Lippolis 9
☎ 080 432 3473 ⓘ Lunch, dinner. Closed Tue (not in Aug), late Jun to mid-Jul

Amalfi Coast

'A Paranza (€€€)
An excellent fish restaurant a few towns up the coast from Amalfi. Try the exquisite *antipasti* (starters) and mixed fried fish *secondo* from which the *trattoria* takes its name (*paranza* means fishing boat).
✉ Via Dragone 1–2, Atrani
☎ 089 871 840 ⓘ Lunch, dinner. Closed Mon in winter, Dec

Bari

La Credenze (€€)
In a well-restored old building in the historic centre, the menu offers Pugliese cuisine including '*ccrude* (raw fish and seafood), grilled vegetables and grilled sausages.
✉ Strada Arco Sant'Onofrio 14
☎ 080 524 4747 ⓘ Dinner only. Closed Mon

Calabrian Coast

A Casa Janca (€€)
An *agriturismo* (► 104) restaurant where fish and seafood from the nearby village alternate with vegetables, chicken, rabbit and pork raised on the farm.
✉ Via Riviera Prangi, Marinella, Pizzo
☎ 0963 264 364 ⓘ Lunch, dinner. Closed Nov, Jan, Feb

Capri

La Rondinella (€€)
Particularly good value in the upper town of this expensive island. A delicious range of mainly fish-based *primi* and *secondi*.
✉ Via G Orlandi 245, Anacapri
☎ 081 837 1223 ⓘ Lunch, dinner. Closed Thu and mid-Jan to mid-Feb

Lecce

Cucina Casereccia (€€)
The name means home cooking, and you'll get the very best in this friendly *trattoria*, whose chef-owner has been invited to New York and Boston to prepare her Lecce specialities.
✉ Via Costadura 9
☎ 0832 245 178 ⓘ Lunch, dinner. Closed Sun dinner, Mon, 30 Aug–15 Sep

Matera

Il Terrazzino sui Sassi (€€)
Excellent views over the *sassi* from this restaurant, itself partially excavated from the rocks. Much use is made of vegetables and pulses in a vast selection of local *primi*, followed by meat, offal or cheese *secondi*.
✉ Vico San Giuseppe 7
☎ 0835 332 503 ⓘ Lunch, dinner. Closed Tue

Naples

Castello (€)
Simply furnished *trattoria* with an interesting menu of vegetable- and fish-based Neapolitan dishes. *Messanelli alla Castello* is pasta with courgettes, ham, basil and cheese.
✉ Via Santa Teresa a Chiaia 38
☎ 081 400 486 ⓘ Dinner, (lunch Sat only). Closed Sun, Aug

La Chiaccierata (€€)
Friendly *trattoria* near Palazzo Reale with authentic Neapolitan cuisine and

atmosphere. Booking recommended for Friday evening, when there is a particularly good *menu degustazione* (► 95).
✉ Piazza Matilde Serao 37 ☎ 081 411 465 🕑 Lunch and Fri dinner. Closed Sat and Sun (Jun–Sep), Aug

Paestum

La Pergola (€€)

Buffalo-milk mozzarella cheese is among the *antipasti* that are followed by fish, cheese and vegetable *primi*. *Pesce spada* (swordfish) on a bed of onions is a house speciality.
✉ Via Nazionale ☎ 0828 723 377 🕑 Lunch, dinner. Closed Mon in winter

Sardinia

Da Gesuino (€€)

The less squeamish should try *asinello* (donkey meat) at this traditional Sassari *trattoria*. Otherwise enjoy *gnocchi sardi* (pasta shells) and ravioli stuffed with ricotta in a tomato sauce.
✉ Via Torres 17, Sassari ☎ 079 273 392 🕑 Lunch, dinner. Closed Sun, two weeks in Aug

San Crispino (€€)

Rustic wooden furniture and a friendly atmosphere accompany a rich assortment of Sardinian specialities, including *culingiones* – large ravioli stuffed with potatoes, mint and cheese.
✉ Corso Vittorio Emmanuele 190, Cagliari ☎ 070 651 853 🕑 Lunch, dinner. Closed Mon, Jul or Aug

Sicily

Archimede (€€)

It was in 1935 that the present owner's father opened this classic restaurant, where the Sicilian specialities include spaghetti in squid ink or with salty sea urchins, followed by fish and seafood from the surrounding waters.
✉ Via Gemmellaro 8, Siracusa ☎ 0931 69 701 🕑 Lunch, dinner. Closed Sun in winter

La Brace (€€)

The owners may be foreign (he's Dutch and she's Indonesian) but they have been here for 20 years, long enough to learn how to prepare fresh-tasting Sicilian specialities *come si deve* (how one should) in their elegant little restaurant. Good fixed-price menu.
✉ Via XXV Novembre 10, Cefalù ☎ 0921 423 570 🕑 Lunch, dinner. Closed Mon, 15 Dec–15 Jan

Capricci di Sicilia (€€)

The *primi*, including *pasta con sarde* (pasta in a taste-packed sardine sauce), are the highlights of a consistently good menu of Palermitano favourites. Swordfish and tuna feature among the *secondi*.
✉ Via Istituto Pignatelli 6, Palermo ☎ 091 327 777 🕑 Lunch, dinner. Closed Mon, two weeks in Aug

Mosaici (€€)

Authentic Sicilian country cuisine in the restaurant of a pretty, well-kept hotel; dried tomatoes are followed by dishes such as *pasta alla Norma* (with aubergines and basil), meat, fish, and roast chicken raised on the farm.
✉ Contrada Paratore 11, Piazza Armerina ☎ 0935 685 453 🕑 Lunch, dinner. Closed Nov–Christmas

What's in a Name?

In general, a *trattoria* is an unpretentious, family-run concern, often with a regular clientele of local people who drop in when they don't want to cook for themselves. *Ristoranti* are usually more formal and expensive places for a special occasion. *Osterie* used to be the most basic of all, although now there is little difference between an *osteria* and a *trattoria* (*osterie* may be less likely to expect you to eat more than one course). However, beware: while all the *osterie* mentioned on these pages are genuine, the name has been adopted by some of the most expensive or touristy establishments and is no longer necessarily synonymous with good value.

The Northwest

Prices
Hotel prices vary across Italy but are particularly high in Rome, Venice, Florence and other main tourist centres. The price brackets used here are for a double room – rooms in the mid- and upper range nearly always have private bathrooms. Those in the lower range do not always have private facilities, but nearly all hotels will have at least a few rooms with private bathrooms.
£ = up to €80
££ = €80–130
£££ = more than €130

Cinqueterre

Gianni Franzi (€)
Simple little *pensione* where some rooms have panoramic balconies (but no bathroom). The hotel's restaurant is particularly good and open to non-residents.
✉ Piazza G Marconi 1, Vernazza ☎ 0187 821 003; fax 0187 821 003 🕑 Closed Jan-Mar

Cremona

Astoria (€)
Family-style hotel in the historic centre. Spacious, clean rooms and a restaurant offering good, home cooking to residents only (dinner only).
✉ Via Bordigallo 19 ☎ 0372 461 616; fax 0372 461 810

Genoa

Hotel Bristol Palace (€€€)
Top-class old hotel (although the grandeur is fading a little) with 133 rooms in a fashionable part of the city.
✉ Via XX Settembre 35
☎ 010 592 541;
www.hotelbristolpalace.com

Lago di Como

Grand Hotel Villa Serbelloni (€€€)
Beautiful hotel in a villa on the lakeshore with old-style luxurious living and modern services.
✉ Via Roma 1, Bellagio
☎ 031 950 216;
www.villaserbelloni.it
🕑 Closed Nov–Mar

Mantua

Broletto (€)
Centrally positioned old *palazzo* with simply furnished rooms, some with 16th-century ceilings and all with independent heating.
✉ Via dell'Accademia 1
☎ 0376 223 678; fax 0376 221 297 🕑 Closed 23 Dec–3 Jan

Milan

Gritti (€€)
Close to the Duomo. Well-equipped rooms, all with a bath or shower, mini-bar and hairdryer. Breakfast buffet and garage parking is included in the price.
✉ Piazza Santa Maria Beltrade 1 ☎ 02 801 056; fax 02 8901 099

London (€€)
Basic, good-value friendly hotel near Castell Sforzesco. Not all rooms have a bathroom, and breakfast and garage parking cost extra.
✉ Via Rovello 3
☎ 02 7202 0166; fax 02 805 7037
🕑 Closed Aug, 23 Dec–3 Jan

Pavia

Excelsior (€)
Basic, functional bed- and bathrooms in this good-value hotel near the station. Continental breakfasts are served at the bar (extra charge).
✉ Piazza Stazione 25
☎ 0382 28 596; fax 0382 26 030

Riviera Ligure

Hotel Cavour (€€)
Right in the centre of Rapallo and in walking distance of the sea, this comfortable hotel is perfect for those seeking a relaxing holiday. Appetising Mediterranean cuisine served in the restaurant.
✉ Galleria Raggio 20, Rapallo
☎ 0185 54 040; fax 0185 54 041

Turin

Chelsea (€€)
Quiet, welcoming, family-run hotel in a central position near the Duomo. En-suite rooms and air-conditioning.
✉ Via XX Settembre 79
☎ 011 436 0100;
www.hotelchelsea.it

The Northeast

Bologna

Roma (€€)
Well-run, tranquil hotel in a historic *palazzo* in the heart of the city centre. Comfortable, well-equipped rooms, some with views. Garage parking (extra charge).
✉ Via M D'Azeglio 9
☎ 051 226 322; fax 057 239 909

Dolomites

Fiechter (€)
Small, central hotel. Simple rooms with functional bathrooms. Breakfast (included) served in a Tyrolean-style dining room.
✉ Via Grappoli 15, Bolzano
☎ 0471 978 768; fax 0471 974 803

Padua

Leon Bianco (€€)
Close to the central piazza. All rooms have bathroom and video (good selection, though mostly in Italian). Breakfast on the terrace (in summer) with views over the rooftops.
✉ Piazzetta Pedrocchi 12
☎ 049 875 0814; fax 049 875 6184

Parma

Button (€)
The pleasant entrance and some of the mainly spacious bedrooms have antique furniture. Most rooms have showers, the others have baths.
✉ Via Salina 7 ☎ 0521 208 039; fax 0521 238 783

Rimini

Biancamano (€€)
A hotel near the sea with its own garden and swimming pool. Spacious, comfortable rooms, a good restaurant, and breakfast buffet, which is included in the price.
✉ Via Cappellini 1
☎ 0541 55 491; fax 0541 55 252

Udine

Astoria Italia (€€€)
Luxurious, attractively furnished hotel in an elegant, historic *palazzo*. Excellent restaurant, pretty garden and bathrooms in all the rooms.
✉ Piazza XX Settembre 24
☎ 0432 505 091; www.hotelastoria.udine.it

Venice

Gritti Palace (€€€)
A dream hotel in a 15th-century *palazzo* on the Grand Canal; one of the best, most luxurious and expensive in Venice. Antique furniture, marble bathrooms, perfect service, private boat to the airport and free transport to a private beach on the Lido.
✉ Campo Santa Maria del Giglio 2467 ☎ 041 794 611; www.luxurycollection.com/grittipalace

Serenissima (€€)
Just behind Piazza San Marco. Simple yet comfortable little hotel where most rooms have bathrooms.
✉ San Marco 4486, Calle Goldoni ☎ 041 520 0011; www.hotelserenissima.it
Closed mid-Nov to mid-Feb (except Christmas)

Wildner (€€€)
Family-run hotel with wonderful terrace overlooking the Riva degli Schiavoni, a view shared by some rooms.
✉ Riva degli Schiavoni 4161
☎ 041 522 7463; fax 041 526 5615

Verona

Bologna (€€)
A 13th-century building near the Arena with comfortable rooms, all with bathrooms. Excellent restaurant.
✉ Via A Mario 18 ☎ 045 800 6830; fax 045 801 0602

Booking
Unless you come to Italy well out of season, it is always advisable to book accommodation in advance. This can be done over the telephone – in more touristy places you may be asked for a deposit (a credit card will usually, but not always, be enough). If you decide not to book, the local EPT office should have a list of all the hotels in the area and you may be able to find something at the last moment.

North Central Italy

Special Needs
Italian culture and society may not take much formal note of special requirements, but the flexibility and initiative of the people means you could encounter extraordinary gestures of generosity (alternatively, you may find your path irredeemably blocked). For example, hotels with no night porter often provide a key for guests who want to stay out late.

Unfortunately, the old *palazzi* which house many hotels do not lend themselves to wheelchairs; but whatever the official line on guests with disabilities, check with the individual establishment first.

Elba

Villa Ombrosa (€€)
Panoramic sun terrace. Many bedrooms have balconies overlooking the beach. Breakfast (not included) and lunch on the terrace.
✉ Via A de Gasperi 3, Portoferraio ☎ 0565 914 363; 0565 915 672

Florence

Helvetia e Bristol (€€€)
Perfectly placed for main Florence sights, this luxury hotel is decorated with 17th-century paintings; bedrooms have antique furniture and jacuzzis. Super bar, top-quality restaurant.
✉ Via dei Pescioni 2 ☎ 055 287 814 or toll-free 1670; fax 055 288 353

Splendour (€€)
In a historic *palazzo* with antique furniture and frescoed walls. Restored, comfortable rooms. Breakfast buffet included.
✉ Via San Gallo 30 ☎ 055 483 427; fax 055 461 276

Gubbio

Bosone Palace (€€)
Excellent value in a 17th-century *palazzo* with antique furniture in the individually decorated bedrooms (all with bath). Nearby restaurant, the Taverna del Lupo, is owned by the same proprietor.
✉ Via XX Settembre 22 ☎ 075 9220 6988; fax 075 922 0552 🕑 Closed Feb

Orvieto

Italia (€€)
A 19th-century building in the historic centre with fine public rooms and functional bedrooms (quieter ones face on to an internal courtyard).
✉ Via del Popolo 13 ☎ 0763 342 065; fax 0763 342 902 🕑 Closed mid-Jan to mid-Feb

Perugia

Priori (€)
Central position. Well-furnished public areas and bedrooms. Breakfast is served on the panoramic terrace during the summer.
✉ Via Vermiglioli 3 ☎ 075 572 3378; www.perugia.com/hotelpriori

Pisa

La Pace (€)
Conveniently close to the station. Family-run hotel in slightly anonymous surroundings. Simple well-equipped rooms; breakfast included.
✉ Viale Gramsci 14, Galleria B ☎ 050 29351

Siena

Duomo (€€)
Well placed for Siena's main sights, with excellent views. Simply furnished rooms have safes and baths. Breakfast included.
✉ Via Stalloreggi 38 ☎ 0577 289 088; www.hotelduomo.it

Spoleto

Aurora (€)
Right next to the Roman theatre, this simple yet comfortable hotel is courteously run. Restaurant.
✉ Via dell'Apollinare 3 ☎ 0743 220 315; www.hotelauroraspoleto.it

Urbino

Bonconte (€€)
Peaceful townhouse hotel with antique furniture and comfortable bed- and bathrooms. Excellent breakfast buffet (included).
✉ Via delle Mura 28 ☎ 0722 2463; fax 0722 4782

South Central Italy

Abruzzo National Park

Paradiso (€)

Unpretentious family hotel perfectly placed for the Parco Nazionale. Good home cooking in the restaurant.

✉ Via Fonte Fracassi 4, Pescasseroli ☎ 0863 910 422; www.albergo-paradiso.it
Closed most of Nov

Castelli Romani

Europa (€)

Traditional hotel in an old, restored building. The bright rooms have views, simple furnishings and bathrooms, and there's a friendly atmosphere.

✉ Piazza della Repubblica 20, Rocca di Papa ☎ 06 9474 9361

Etruria

Al Gallo (€€)

Delightful little hotel in Tuscania's historic centre with antiques among its tasteful furnishings. Good breakfast included in the price. The hotel's restaurant is one of the best in the area.

✉ Via del Gallo 22, Tuscania
☎ 0761 443 388; www.algallo.it

Rome

Campo dei Fiori (€€)

In one of the loveliest quarters of the capital's centre, this hotel (terrace overlooks Roman rooftops) is in a flaking ochre-coloured street. Pleasant décor and multilingual staff.

✉ Via dei Biscione 6
☎ 06 6880 6865; fax 06 687 6003

Esquilino (€€)

On the 'clean' side of the station. This lovingly refurbished hotel is run by two professional hoteliers. Some rooms look out at Santa Maria Maggiore but the courtyard is quieter.

✉ Piazza dell'Esquilino 29
☎ 06 474 3454

Hassler Villa Medici (€€€)

One of the grandest old-style luxury hotels in the heart of an elegant part of the city (above the Spanish Steps). There's a view to die for from the stunning roof terrace and restaurant.

✉ Piazza Trinità dei Monti 6
☎ 06 699 340; www.hotelhasslerroma.com

Perugia (€€)

The staff at the Perugia are friendly and multilingual and most of the 13 rooms have bathrooms. Breakfast included. Just two steps from the Colosseum.

✉ Via del Colosseo 7
☎ 06 679 7200; fax 06 678 4635

Portoghesi (€€)

Tucked away in a lovely side street in one of the prettiest areas, near Piazza Navona. Tastefully furnished.

✉ Via dei Portoghesi 1
☎ 06 686 4231; www.hotelportoghesiroma.com

Sant'Anselmo (€€)

A lovely, reasonably priced hotel in a villa with garden on the peaceful Aventine hill behind ancient Rome.

✉ Piazza Sant'Anselmo 2
☎ 06 574 5174; www.aventinohotels.com

Trastevere (€€)

Excellent value in renovated rooms in one of the best parts of the city for nightlife. Loft-style self-catering apartments sleeping up to four on the top floor.

✉ Via L Manara 24a
☎ 06 581 4713; fax 06 5881 1016

The Cost of a Star

The Italian star rating system can make it difficult to know what you are getting, as it is based exclusively on facilities offered. This means, for example, a charmingly furnished atmospheric 2-star affair may cost less than a run-down 3-star establishment. This is further complicated by the fact that fewer stars mean less tax, with some hoteliers happy not to upgrade themselves.

The South

Rural Accommodation
Agriturismo is a growing business offering a wide range of holiday accommodation in the country, usually on operating or former farms. *Agriturismi* are sometimes fairly basic rooms in a house shared with the owners. Others are of the standard of luxury hotels and some offer independent apartments or cottages in the grounds. Most have some sort of restaurant providing excellent local food and wines at competitive prices and some have swimming pools, tennis courts and other sports facilities. A range of activity holidays varies from cookery to art history to horse-riding. To find out what's on offer, contact Agriturist (✉ Corso Vittorio Emanuele 101, Roma 00186 ☎ 06 685 2342) which publishes *Agriturismo e Vacanze Verdi*.

Alberobello

Dei Trulli (€€€)
Live in your own *trullo*, furnished in Mediterranean style, in a pretty park with restaurant, swimming pool and children's playground.
✉ **Via Cadore 29**
☎ **080 432 3555; www.inmedia.it/hoteldeitrulli**

Amalfi Coast

Giordano (€€)
Simple, comfortable bedrooms and a friendly atmosphere in this little hotel surrounded by greenery. Facilities include a swimming pool.
✉ **Via Santa Trinità 14, Ravello**
☎ **089 857 255; fax 089 857 071**
Closed Nov–Mar

Gargano

Seggio (€)
Well-run hotel in Vieste's 17th-century former town hall right next to the sea. Rooms with bath, private beach, swimming pool and restaurant. In Aug, minimum stay one week (full board).
✉ **Via Veste 7, Vieste**
☎ **0884 708 123; fax 0884 470 8727** **Closed Nov–Dec**

Lecce

Risorgimento (€€)
This building in the historic centre has been an inn since the 17th century. Elegantly furnished bedrooms with bath; some have private terrace. Breakfast included.
✉ **Via Augusto Imperatore 19**
☎ **0832 242 125**

Naples

Cavour (€€)
Top-floor hotel near the station with attractive terrace and spacious, simple rooms (air-conditioning extra; breakfast included). Good fixed price menu in the restaurant.
✉ **Piazza Garibaldi 32**
☎ **081 283 122**

Vesuvio (€€€)
Elegant, luxury hotel with views over Porta Santa Lucia. Stylish décor and antique furnishings. Two restaurants. Superb rooms include some with child-sized furniture. Sports club, sauna and limousine service.
✉ **Via Partenope 45** ☎ **081 764 0044; fax 081 764 4483**

Sardinia

Leonardo da Vinci (€€€)
In a central position near Sassari's archaeology museum. Spacious, modern bedrooms; suitable for families. Breakfast (not included) on the terrace.
✉ **Via Roma 79, Sassari**
☎ **079 280 744; www.leonardodavincihotel.it**

Sicily

Domus Mariae (€€)
Beautifully restored old building in Syracuse's historic centre, near the sea. Excellent service, library, period furniture and a piano. Spacious well-equipped rooms, elegant marble bathrooms. Inclusive breakfast buffet.
✉ **Via Vittorio Veneto 76, Siracusa** ☎ **0931 24 854; fax 0931 24 858**

Grande Albergo Sole (€€)
Large, central hotel well-placed for sightseeing. Spacious, tastefully furnished bedrooms (those on the street are a little noisy). Access to private beach during the summer.
✉ **Corso Vittorio Emmanuele 291, Palermo** ☎ **091 604 1111**

Crafts, Gifts & Souvenirs

The Northeast

Laboratorio artigianale maschere

Some of the most unusual and spectacular masks in Venice, made, as they have been for centuries, for masked balls and parties during *Carnevale*.

✉ Barbaria delle Tole, Castello 6657, Venezia
☎ 041 522 3110

Paolo Olbi

Massive, ever-changing range of traditional marbled and dragged Venetian papers used to cover luxurious notebooks, diaries and desk accessories.

✉ Calle della Mandola, San Marco 3653, Venezia
☎ 041 528 5025

Venini

One of the most famous of Venice's many glassware shops. Exquisite pieces with prices to match.

✉ Piazzetta dei Leoncini 314, San Marco, Venezia
☎ 041 522 4045

North Central Italy

Farmacia di Santa Maria Novella

Old-world apothecary in Florence selling its own herbal elixirs, soaps and other concoctions, made to old monks' recipes. Branches in other Italian cities.

✉ Via della Scala 16, Firenze
☎ 055 216 276/055 288 658

South Central Italy

Spazio Sette

Not cheap, but quite easily the best home shop in central Rome, selling everything from glassware to hardware, postcards to furniture; all stamped with unmistakable Italian design.

✉ Via dei Barbieri 7, Roma
☎ 06 6880 4261

The South

Associazione figle d'arte Cuticchio

Workshop which makes traditional Sicilian puppets used in the attached puppet theatre. Takes special orders.

✉ Via Bara all'Olivella 95, Palermo ☎ 091 323 400

Mostra Permanente dell'Artigianato

Crafts from all over Salento, including Leccese papier mâché, homely Pugliese ceramics, handmade lace and wrought iron.

✉ Via Rubichi, Lecce
☎ 0832 246 758

Nativity scenes

The streets around Via San Gregorio Armeno in Naples are full of little shops and stalls selling figures for traditional nativity scenes and others of famous personalities of the year.

✉ Side streets around Via San Gregorio Armeno, Napoli

Pustorino

One of Palermo's oldest shops, famous for handmade ties, which are made to measure and sent all over the world.

✉ Via Maqueda 174, Palermo

De Simone

Vibrant-coloured Sicilian ceramics painted with typically Palermitano motifs and designs. Not the cheapest around but excellent quality.

✉ Piazza Leoni 2, Palermo

Opening and Closing

Shop opening hours are changing with more all-day and Sunday openings, especially in the main cities and tourist centres. Generally, however, it is a Monday to Saturday set-up with a break from 1 to 5PM. Food shops close on Thursday afternoon and others on Monday morning (Saturday afternoon during the summer)

Fashion & Accessories

Italian Designer Fashion

Milan is the business and spiritual centre for most top Italian designers, although a few (among them Valentino) are based in Rome and one or two elsewhere. In any case, all the big names of Italian and foreign designer fashion have branches in both Milan and Rome, and most Italian towns of any size or importance will have a good sprinkling of designer clothes shops.

The Northwest

Armani

The prince of essential, classic, understated Italian style is based in Milan but, like all the top designers, has branches all over Italy.

✉ Via Sant'Andrea 31, Milano ☎ 02 7231 8600

Dolce e Gabbana

Particularly popular with the style-conscious youth, Dolce and Gabbana's dramatic yet wearable styles use distinctive printed fabrics and strong colours.

✉ Via della Spiga 2, Milano ☎ 02 7600 1155

Fiorucci

The Milanese designer who rose to fame for his young, American-influenced styles has expanded his empire to include clothes for all ages and a massive range of personal and household accessories.

✉ Galleria Passerella 1, Milano ☎ 02 7600 3276

Prada

Currently the most popular Italian designer among the international fashion set. Clothes which combine elegance with opulent quirkiness are accompanied by the classy shoes, bags and accessories with which Prada first rose to fame.

✉ Via Montenapoleone 6/8, Milano ☎ 02 7602 0273

Versace

The man may have passed away (murdered in Florida in 1997) but the name, famous for over-the-top extravagance and drama, lives on.

✉ Via Montenapoleone 2, Milano ☎ 02 7600 8529

North Central Italy

Emilio Pucci

Florence's own designer is famous for his 1960s-style clothes. You need an appointment to visit the showroom at the family palace, but the shop is open normal hours.

✉ Via della Vigna Nuova 97–9, Firenze ☎ 055 294 028

South Central Italy

Arsenale

Owner Patrizia Pieroni's outlet for her own romantic designs, which are an interesting mix of classic and original, incorporating the most wonderful velvets, silks, linens and lace.

✉ Via del Governo Vecchio 64, Roma ☎ 06 686 1380

Gucci

Mouthwatering classics are on offer at this chic Italian designer's outlets.

✉ Via Condotti 8, Roma ☎ 06 678 9340

Max Mara

The affordable end of designer land. Max Mara offers wonderfully crisp shapes and clean colours in its many outlets.

✉ Via Nazionale 28–31, Roma ☎ 06 488 5870

Valentino

Rome's own designer has his boutique in Via Condotti, just two doors from the wonderful headquarters in Piazza Mignatelli. The casual wear outlet, Oliver, is round the corner on Via del Babuino.

✉ Via Condotti 13, Roma ☎ 06 678 3656

Food & Drink, Flea Markets & Leather

Food and Drink

The Northeast

Pasticceria Marchini
Venice's best *pasticceria* emits mouthwatering smells and has a massive selection of traditional cakes, chocolates and other confectionery.
Ponte San Maurizio, Venezia **041 522 9109**

North Central Italy

Enoteca San Lorenzo
Wide selection of wines from Umbria and other Italian regions.
Via San Lorenzo 1, Todi
075 894 400

South Central Italy

Ai Monasteri
Seven monasteries all send their produce for sale to this shop just behind Piazza Navona. Honey, liqueurs, preserves and ranges of natural toiletries and skin products are available.
Corso Rinascimento 72, Roma **06 6880 2783**

Markets

North Central Italy

Mercato delle Pulci
Florence's flea market sells antiques and *bric à brac* on weekdays and is particularly extensive on the last Sunday of every month (except July).
Piazza dei Ciompi, Firenze

South Central Italy

Porta Portese
Rome's flea market is famous throughout Italy. It takes over the streets near Trastevere every Sunday morning and is jam-packed. You can buy almost anything imaginable from clothes (beware of fake labels) to books and antiques.
Via Porta Portese, Roma

The South

Mercato della Vucciria
Palermo's lively, cluttered food market (every morning except Sunday) is one of the most painted, filmed and written about in Italy.
Piazza Caracciolo and surrounding streets

Shoes and Leather

The Northeast

Risuolatutto di Gianni Dittura
A wide variety of traditonal, brightly coloured Venetian velour slippers, called *furlanette*.
San Vio, Dorsoduro 871
041 523 1163

North Central Italy

Salvatore Ferragamo
Among the most sought-after shoes in the world have been made by the same Florentine family since the 1940s.
Via de'Tornabuoni 16, Firenze **055 292 123**

South Central Italy

Fausto Santini
The ultimate in Roman shoe design, Fausto Santini's styles are original and elegant and you won't find anything quite like them elsewhere.
Via Frattina 120, Roma
06 678 4114

Top Ten Buys
The top ten things to buy (and where to buy them) are:
- Ceramics (Sicily, Puglia, northeast and north central Italy)
- Chocolate (Turin)
- Designer fashion (Milan and Rome)
- Glassware (Venice)
- Olive oil (Tuscany)
- Paper and stationery (Florence and Venice)
- Religious memorabilia (Vatican, Rome; Naples for nativity scenes)
- Shoes and leather (Milan, Rome, Venice and north central Italy)
- Traditional toys, puppets, dolls, figures (south Italy)
- Wines (Tuscany and northeast Italy)

Outdoor & Indoor Fun

Aquaparks
In summer, water parks open up along the coast and at many inland holiday centres. Aimed principally at young families, these have swimming and paddling pools with wave machines, and usually several waterslides of varying degrees of excitement to serve all ages and levels of courage. Most have bar and/or restaurant facilities, a land-based play park and sometimes a few funfair-type rides and attractions.

The Northwest

Acquario di Genova
Europe's biggest aquarium; two dolphins, Bonnie and Cleo, are among the main attractions.
✉ Piazza Caricamento, Genova ☎ 010 248 1205

Città dei Bambini
Strictly for 3- to 14-year-olds (and accompanying adults), this area of vaguely educational games and attractions includes a house in construction, a TV studio and a massive anthill.
✉ Magazzini del Cotone, Genova ☎ 010 247 5702

The Northeast

Archimede Seguso
Take the children to watch Venetian glass being made in this traditional factory. Prices are high, but there's a range of appealing souvenirs at pocket-money prices.
✉ Fondamento Vetrai 28, Murano, Venezia
☎ 041 739 049

Fiabilandia
A theme park directed firmly towards children, with rides into a giant apple, to the lake of dreams and into a mine in the Grand Canyon. There is also a puppet and model museum and a vast swimming pool.
✉ Via Cardano, Rivazzurra, Rimini ☎ 0541 372 064

Gardaland
Italy's biggest and best theme park has 23 attractions, 11 shows and 4 theme villages, including vertiginous rides for the strong of stomach, a pirates' galleon, a treasure hunt with Indiana Jones in ancient Egypt, and villages of the Caribbean and the Wild West.
✉ Località Ronchi, Castelnuovo del Garda
☎ 045 644 9777

Italia in Miniatura
All the most famous architectural and natural sights of Italy, at a scale of 1:25 or 1:50, many of them with moving parts and (minute) transport systems that seem to function better than the real thing. Some of the great sights of the rest of Europe are also here.
✉ Via Popilia 239, Viserba, Rimini ☎ 0541 732 004

Mirabilandia
A massive theme park divided into eight distinct areas catering for all ages. *L'Evolution* is the biggest transportable big wheel in the world (35m high).
✉ S S Adriatica Km 162, Savio (between Rimini and Ravenna)
☎ 0544 561 111

Museo Storico Navale
Models and exhibits tracing the history of the Venetian and Italian navies include a replica of the Doge's ceremonial barge and World War II torpedoes.
✉ Campo dell'Arsenale, Venezia ☎ 041 520 0276

North Central Italy

Città della Domenica
As well as a zoo and reptile house, 'Sunday City' has a few imaginative rides and themed attractions including Tarzan's house, Sleeping Beauty's castle, the Wooden Horse of Troy, and a maze.
✉ Località Monte Pulito, Perugia ☎ 075 505 4941

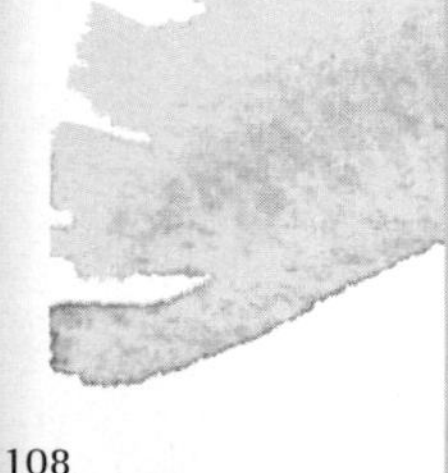

Museo Leonardiano
The castle in the town of Leonardo da Vinci's birth contains models of the great master's inventions taken from his notebooks; they include an armoured tank, a car and water-skis.
✉ **Castello dei Conti Guido, Vinci, Toscana** ☎ **0571 56 055**

Parco di Pinocchio
The story of Pinocchio is told through a series of scenes reconstructing the most important events with models. There is also a small theme park area.
✉ **Via San Gennaro 3, Collodi, Tuscany** ☎ **0572 429 342 and 429 613**

South Central Italy

Biopark
Rome's renamed and much improved zoo in the Villa Borghesi has a good range of animals and play areas for children of all ages. Many of the inmates are housed in new, well-designed habitats and there are plans to improve more in the future.
✉ **Viale del Giardino Zoologico 1** ☎ **06 320 1912**

Luna Park
Slightly shabby funfair, more than 30 years old, with good, old-fashioned fun for all the family.
✉ **Via delle Tre Fontane, Roma** ☎ **06 592 5933**

Museo della Civiltà Romano
Models and reconstructions show what life was like in ancient Rome. There's a huge model of the ancient city in the 4th century AD.
✉ **Piazza Gianni Agnelli 10, EUR, Roma** ☎ **06 592 6135**

Museo del Folklore e dei Poeti Romaneschi
Reconstructed rooms and street scenes, peopled with dummies in costume, show what Rome looked like in the 17th and 18th centuries.
✉ **Piazza San Egidio 1, Roma** ☎ **06 581 6563**

Sacro Bosco Parco dei Mostri
Not far from Rome these surreal stone sculptures of monsters were sculpted for an eccentric Renaissance prince in the mid-16th century. Also a mini-zoo with peacocks, deer and goats.
✉ **Località Giardino, Sacro Bosco Bomarzo, near Viterbo** ☎ **0761 924 029**

The South

Edenlandia
A theme park packed with a massive range of fairly standard rides and attractions based on, among other themes, the Wild West, historic China, life in a castle and science fiction.
✉ **Viale Kennedy, Napoli** ☎ **081 239 9693**

Etna
For a real adventure take a trip up Sicily's live volcano. These are organised from Catania, Taormina or Linguaglossa and, although they don't come cheap, they're a memorable experience, particularly at night. Trips are subject to cancellation for bad weather or volcanic activity.
✉ **Largo Paisello 5, Catania** ☎ **095 312 124 or** ✉ **Piazza Santa Caterina, Taormina** ☎ **0942 23 243 or** ✉ **Piazza Annunziata 5, Linguaglossa** ☎ **095 643 094**

Christmas
Christmas decorations in Italy are comparatively understated, with many (but by no means all) historic centres going in for tasteful lighting effects, red carpets and pretty plant-based arrangements rather than kilowatt-guzzling displays of cartoon characters. Churches all over the country open their doors to display their *presepi* (nativity scenes), often with valuable old models placed in realistic Renaissance street scenes. There are special Christmas markets in many town centres selling figures for nativity scenes, cheap toys and garish sweets.

Festivals & Seasons

Sagre – Food and Wine Festivals

Small towns and villages all over Italy hold festivals to celebrate their local speciality. Most of these take place in spring, early and late summer and autumn, when you can gorge on strawberries, mushrooms, truffles, apples and a host of other things depending on where you are. The year's new wines (*vini novelli*) are released in mid-November and you can sample these at special celebrations organised by town councils, wine bars and restaurants. Information about local *sagre* is available from tourist offices.

The Northwest

Festival Arturo Benedetti Michelangeli

This important piano festival was founded in 1964 and is named after Arturo Benedetti Michelangeli, the pianist who was born in Bergamo. Over the years it has seen the best of established pianists and orchestras as well as fresh new talent. It runs throughout May and June.

Information: Bergamo ☎ 035 240 140 or Brescia ☎ 030 993 022

The Northeast

Biennale di Venezia

Every second year (odd numbers), from June to September, Venice hosts the world's biggest exhibition of contemporary art, where each participating country has its own semi-permanent pavilion in which to exhibit the works of its best artists.

The Venice Film Festival, one of the most important showcases in the world for new films, is held every year in the Venice Lido. It runs from late August through to early September, and attracts luminaries of the international movie scene.

☎ www.labiennale.org

Festival Arena di Verona

In July and August the 1st-century AD Roman theatre is the evocative setting for good-quality productions of popular operas. Although the performances are aimed at the tourists who flock here in their thousands, opera buffs usually find little to complain about in the productions.

✉ Piazza Brà, Verona
☎ 045 800 5151

Festival di Cremona Claudio Monteverdi

Cremona honours its most famous son in May and early July with concerts of music by his successors to the present day.

Information: ☎ 0372 407 274; www.rccr.cremona.it

Ravenna Festival

International conductor and Ravenna resident, Riccardo Muti, is the guiding light behind this festival of music, opera and dance performed in the stunning settings of the city's old basilicas and *palazzi* from mid-June to late July.

Information: ☎ 0544 249 211

North Central Italy

Festival ei Due Mondi

Italian-American composer Gian Carlo Menotti (who was born in Spoleto) started the by now world-famous Festival of Two Worlds in the 1950s. Since then, the last week of June and the first two of July see every available corner of Spoleto being used to host performances by top international opera, music, dance and theatre companies. There are also puppet shows, exhibitions, cinema and science displays.

Information: ✉ Teatro Nuovo, Spoleto ☎ 0743 4700; www.spoletofestival.it

Macerata Opera

This long-established festival in one of Italy's oldest university towns (in Le Marche) is a chance to see good-quality opera favourites in the Arena Sferisterio. This outdoor

theatre has surprisingly good acoustics considering that it was built as a sports stadium in the early 19th century. It runs from late July to mid-August.
☎ **0733 230 735**

Maggio Musicale Fiorentino

Florence's annual festival of music, opera and dance takes place in late April and early July and has been running for more than 60 years. Some of the world's best conductors, directors, choreographers and performers come to work with the specially formed Orchestra del Maggio Musicale and MaggioDanza and there are top-class international visiting companies as well.
Information: ✉ Teatro Comunale, Corso Italia 16, Firenze ☎ 055 211 158; wwwmaggiofiorentino.com

Rossini Opera Festival

Pesaro in Le Marche celebrates its most famous son; the opera composer Gioacchino Rossini, with a festival dedicated to his music for two weeks in August.
Information: ☎ 0721 30161

Torre del Lago

The lakeside home of composer Giacomo Puccini (1858–1924) near Viareggio in northern Tuscany, where he composed many of his most famous works, is the atmospheric setting for a festival of his operatic and orchestral works, held in the first half of August.
✉ Piazza Belvedere Puccini, Torre del Lago, Lucca ☎ 0584 350 567

Umbria Jazz

Italy's most important jazz festival attracts big names of classic and contemporary jazz from all over the world for about ten days in mid-July. Concerts, parades and jam sessions are held in Perugia and in many of the towns and villages round about. There is also a mini-Umbria Jazz festival held over the New Year.
Information: ☎ 075 572 1155

South Central Italy

Estate Romano

Rome becomes festival city during the summer with festivals dedicated to cinema, music of all kinds, theatre, opera, dance and other more specialist themes; many of the performances are held at attractive outdoor venues. The biggest of these concurrent festivals is Romaeuropa, which runs on through the autumn with a mass of music, dance and theatre from local, national and international performers. Information from tourist offices and booths throughout the city, or try the website given below.
Information: ✉ Fondazione Romaeuropa ☎ www.romaeuropa.net

The South

Taormina Arte

The ancient Greek theatre, with its stunning views over the sea and of Mount Etna, is the fabulous setting for music, theatre and dance performances throughout July and early August.
✉ Teatro Greco, Via Teatro Greco ☎ 0942 21 142

Terme di Caracalla

For many years the remains of Caracalla's baths (3rd century AD) in Rome made a perfect setting for summer opera productions, which were staged in the hot-bath area. Over recent years, wrangling between the town council and Rome's opera company put a stop to this and now summer opera is nomadic, with venues that range from the sublime Piazza di Spagna in Villa Borghese to the ridiculous Stadio Olimpico football pitch. All is not lost, however, and every year attempts are made to re-establish opera at the baths. In the meantime these are used for concerts and other events. Summer opera
☎ 06 481 601

Opera, Ballet, Theatre & Classical Music

Finding Out What's On
This guide lists just a few of the venues available in Italy's main cities. Every town in Italy has a good range of cultural events, often performed in beautiful historic settings. The local press and publicity posters are the best sources of finding out what's on where. Tourist offices and town councils also publish information, but the best-laid plans often change at the last minute in Italy, so treat these with caution.

The Northwest

Teatro Piccolo
Milan's main theatre is also one of the best in Italy for traditional productions of Italian and foreign classics (in Italian).

Via Rovello 2, Milano
02 7233 3222

Teatro alla Scala
The most famous opera house in the world opened its doors in 1778 and has gone from strength to strength ever since, attracting the most sumptuous and (occasionally) original productions and the biggest names of opera. The Museo Teatrale has sets and costumes from La Scala's productions and a good view of the auditorium for those who fail to get their hands on tickets, which are sold out months in advance.

Piazza della Scala, Milano 02 7200 3744. Museo Teatrale 02 887 9473

The Northeast

La Fenice
Venice's opera house was almost completely destroyed by fire in 1996. While a massive restoration project is under way, opera and ballet performances take place at the semi-permanent Palafenice.

Tronchetto, Venezia
041 786 582

North Central Italy

Teatro Comunale
During the winter, the headquarters of Maggio Musicale Fiorentino (➤ 111) is used for classical music concerts, opera and ballet.

South Central Italy

Auditorio di Santa Cecilia
The Accademia has among Rome's best chamber and symphony orchestras, which perform here during the winter and in the glorious outdoor setting of Villa Giulia in the summer.

Via della Conciliazione 4, Roma 06 6880 1044

Teatro Agorà
This theatre hosts visiting theatre companies from the rest of Europe. Plays are in Italian, English, French, Spanish and so on, depending on who is here.

Via della Penitenza 33, Roma 06 687 4167

Teatro Argentina
This beautifully restored 19th-century theatre is one of the homes of the Italian National Theatre, which stages good, traditional performances of classic plays. In summer they move to the Roman theatre at Ostia Antica (➤ 81).

Largo di Torre Argentina 52, Roma 06 6880 4601

The South

Teatro San Carlo
During the 19th century Naples was the capital of opera and its theatre (built next to the Palazzo Reale in the mid-18th century) owes much of its present appeance to an early 19th-century refurbishment following a fire. Its prestigious opera company still regards itself as superior to all, including La Scala.

Via San Carlo, Napoli
081 797 2412

Nightlife

The Northwest

Bar Magenta
Long established as Milan's perfect setting for an aperitif or late-night drink.
✉ **Via Carducci 13, Milano**
☎ **02 805 3808**

Barrumba
The best and visiting DJs in Turin as well as some interesting visiting groups.
✉ **Via San Massimo 1, Torino**
☎ **011 883 322**

Docks Dora
An old industrial estate is the setting for alternative music, cinema, other performances and lively parties.
✉ **Via Valprato 68, Torino**
☎ **011 280 251**

Hollywood
The place to people-watch, frequented by models, sports people and big names from the Milan fashion scene.
✉ **Corso Como 15, Milano**
☎ **02 659 8996**

Plastic
Open till late with Milan's best DJs and a loyal, vaguely alternative clientele.
✉ **Viale Umbria 120, Milano**
☎ **02 733 996**

Shocking Club
Avant-garde venue for garage, hip-hop, house and underground, where Milan's sophisticated youth come to hang out at weekends.
✉ **Via Bastioni di Porta Nuova 12, Milano** ☎ **02 655 1240**

The Northeast

Florian
Café founded on Piazza San Marco by Florian Francesconi in 1720; a pianist plays soothing music as you sip extortionately priced drinks in, admittedly, unique surroundings.
✉ **Piazza San Marco 56, Venezia** ☎ **041 525 5641**

Harry's Bar
The most famous bar in Italy was founded in 1931 by Giuseppe Cipriani and has been frequented by generations of Venice's famous visitors. It's still *the* place for cocktails, but the restaurant is a bit overpriced.
✉ **Calle Vallaresso 1323, Venezia** ☎ **041 528 5777**

Paradiso Perduto
Arty bar-cum-eatery with regular live music (for which the bar prices are increased).
✉ **Fondamenta della Misericordia 2540, Venezia**
☎ **041 720 581**

North Central Italy

Auditorium Flog
This is where the best and most famous jazz and rock musicians come to play in Florence. Open only for concerts.
✉ **Via Mercati 24, Firenze**
☎ **055 490 437**

Cabiria
Its beautiful setting with outside tables attracts Florentines and visitors alike.
✉ **Piazza Santo Spirito 4, Firenze** ☎ **055 215 732**

Jazz Club
Drinks and snacks accompany concerts or other musical events most evenings at this historic haunt of Florence's jazz *aficionados*.
✉ **Via Nuova de'Cacci 3**
☎ **055 247 9700**

Cinema: *Lingua Originale*
Italy is proud of its dubbing tradition, which is bad news for anybody wanting to see films in languages other than Italian. However, there are cinemas in many major towns and cities that show films in their original language (*lingua originale*) – usually English – on at least one day a week. In Rome, Cinema Pasquino (✉ Piazza San Egidio ☎ 06 580 3622) has three screens all dedicated to showing films in English, usually with Italian subtitles.

Adriatic Clubland
The Adriatic coast around Rimini and Riccione becomes Italy's clubbing capital during the summer, when holidaymakers flock to a plethora of permanent and summer-only indoor and outdoor clubs, where guest DJs, organisers and artists from all over the world make sure they have a night to remember. During the summer a special bus, the Blue Line, operates along the coast carrying ravers and partygoers to and from the clubs all through the night. Details of the Rimini club scene are in the fortnightly *Chiamami Città*.

Meccanò
The best and busiest disco in Florence.
✉ **Piazza Vittorio Veneto, Firenze** ☎ **055 331 371**

Rivoire
A beautiful marble interior and tables on Piazza Signoria make this a compulsory (if expensive) spot for an evening drink or aperitif.
✉ **Piazza Signoria 5r, Firenze**
☎ **055 214 412**

South Central Italy

Alexanderplatz
Rome's flagship jazz club; the best the capital has to offer.
✉ **Via Ostia 9, Roma**
☎ **06 3974 2171**

Alpheus
Three separate areas: one for jazz, one for rock and the other for dancing to records.
✉ **Via del Commercio 36, Roma** ☎ **06 574 7826**

Big Mama
Sub-titled 'the home of the blues in Rome', Big Mama has an interesting programme of live music performed by Italian and international musicians, including the occasional legend.
✉ **Vicolo San Francesco a Ripa 18, Roma** ☎ **06 581 2551**

Gilda
The establishment place to bop (or watch others), frequented by, among others, right-wing politicians and TV personalities.
✉ **Via Mario de'Fiori 97, Roma**
☎ **06 678 4838**

Goa
Bright, lively nightclub with a weekly gay night and lots of house, jungle, tech house and other types of music.
✉ **Via Libetta 13, Roma**
☎ **06 574 8277**

La Vineria
In summer, the clients of this informal little wine bar spill out into Campo de'Fiori. A massive choice of drinks and good prices. Popular with trendy foreigners.
✉ **Campo de'Fiori 15, Roma**
☎ **06 6880 3268**

The South

Gambrinus
Enjoy the night air sitting outside at Naples' most famous café with its pleasant atmosphere of faded splendour.
✉ **Via Chiaia 1, Napoli**
☎ **081 417 582**

Lido Pola
Summertime disco with open-air dancing by the sea, overlooking the island of Nisida. Venue for the occasional rave.
✉ **Via Nisida 34, Napoli**

Riot
Naples' young, alternative crowd flocks to this bar in an old *palazzo* near the Duomo.
✉ **Via San Biagio dei Librai 39, Napoli**

Sottovento
The club where all the glitterati hang out on the Costa Smeralda.
✉ **Porto Cervo, Arzachena**
☎ **06 678 4838**

Villa Giuditta
Disco in the incongruous setting of a 19th-century, aristocratic villa.
✉ **Via San Lorenzo colli 17, Palermo** ☎ **091 688 6256**

Sport

Cycling

The annual Giro d'Italia, in which international cyclists compete in a race around Italy, takes place during the second half of May. If you want to do some cycling yourself, local tourist offices can give you details of routes and/or where to hire equipment.

Football

You can always tell when there's an important football match on because cries of alternating rage and triumph erupt from nearby houses, and the streets are filled with middle-aged men, tiny transistor radios clamped to their ears as they stroll, listening to the frenzied commentary that acts as a sort of soundtrack to the entire day. Needless to say, the atmosphere at the ground is particularly exciting and anybody with any interest in football at all should try to attend a match (buy tickets in advance). Here are a few of the biggest Italian teams:

Juventus (Turin)
✉ **Stadio delle Alpi, Strada Altessano 131, Continassa, Venaria Reale, Torino**
☎ **011 738 0081**

Napoli
✉ **Stadio di San Paolo, Fuorigrotta, Napoli**

Rome and Lazio (both teams)
✉ **Stadio Olimpico, Via del Foro Italico, Roma**
☎ **06 3685 7520**

Inter Milan and AC Milan (both teams)
✉ **Stadio G Meazza, Via Piccoliminni 5, Milano**
☎ **02 4001 1228**

Golf

Federazione Italiana Golf
✉ **Viale Tiziano 74, 00196 Roma** ☎ **06 323 1825**

Horse-riding

Associazione Nazionale per il Turismo Equestre
✉ **Piazza Antonio Manini 4, 00196 Roma** ☎ **06 3265 0230**

Motor Racing

The Italian Formula One Grand Prix is held at Monza, near Milan, in September.

Mountaineering, Hillwalking

Club Alpino Italiano
✉ **Via Silvio Pellico 6, Milano**
☎ **02 8646 3516**

Sailing

Federazione Italiana Vela
✉ **Piazza Bovgo Pila 40, Genova** ☎ **010 544 541**

Swimming and the Beach

A lack of public swimming pools makes the beach your best bet for swimming. Much of the Italian coast has been taken over by entrepreneurs who charge a few thousand lire for access to their patch of beach (*stablimento*), unless you hire a sunbed and parasol from them. This may seem extortionate, but you will usually have access to showers, toilets, changing rooms and volleyball pitches. There is nearly always a bar or restaurant serving drinks and snacks. Some *stablimenti* also have pools and a few have tennis courts and other watersports facilities such as sailboards for hire.

Skiing

In winter you are never very far from a skiing resort (even Rome and Naples are at a weekend travelling distance from the Abruzzi Apennines). The best areas are in the north, particularly Val D'Aosta and the Dolomites. Local tourist offices can tell you where to go and how to get there or try ✉ Federazione Italiana Sport Invernali Via Peranesi 44b, 20137 Milano ☎ 02 75 731

What's On When

Saints' Days
These are only a few of the traditional holidays and feast days that are celebrated in Italy. Most communities also have special religious parades on their patron saint's day, when effigies and relics of the saint and/or the Virgin are taken from their usual resting place in the main church and paraded through the streets in processions of priests, nuns, monks and pilgrims, often in historic costume. These parades usually finish at some significant spot (often in or by the sea in coastal communities) and are followed by general feasting and celebrations.

January
New Year's Day: public holiday.
Epiphany (6 Jan): public holiday. Traditionally the *befana* (witch) leaves presents for children.

February
Week leading up to Shrove Tuesday: *Carnevale*. Streets full of adults and children in fancy dress throwing confetti and firecrackers. Particularly important in Venice.

March/April
Good Friday: Pope leads ceremony of the Stations of the Cross at the Colosseum in Rome (➤ 20).
Easter Sunday: Papal address from San Pietro (➤ 16)
Settimana Beni Culturali (Late Mar–early Apr): a week of free admission and guided tours to state museums and other, infrequently open, monuments.
Rome's birthday (21 Apr): bands and orchestras perform outside, all over the city and there are fireworks at night.
Liberation Day (25 Apr): public holiday to commemorate the Allies' liberation of Italy from the Nazis in 1944.

May
Labour Day (1 May): public holiday. Most places shut and there is very limited public transport.
Festa dei Ceri, Gubbio (5 May)] ➤ 61.

June
Calcio Storico Fiorentino (24 Jun): costume procession, fireworks and a ball game in Piazza della Signoria, Florence.

July
Palio delle Contrade, Siena (2 Jul): costumed participants take part in flag-waving and a fearsome horse race round Piazza del Campo.
Festa della Santa Maria del Carmine, Naples (16 Jul): historic festival featuring illumination of the church of Santa Maria del Carmine.

August
Ferragosto (15 Aug): public holiday. Many shops, restaurants, bars and businesses close for a week or more.
Palio delle Contrade (16 Aug): see 2 July.
Giostra del Saracino, Arezzo (last Sun in Aug): medieval joust.

September
Regata Storica, Venice (first Sun in Sep): procession of historic boats and a gondola race.

November
All Saints' Day (1 Nov): public holiday.
Early Nov: the new season's *vini novelli* (new wines) ready for drinking.

December
Immaculate Conception (8 Dec): public holiday.
Christmas time: *presepi* (nativity scenes) on show in churches.
Christmas Day (25 Dec): public holiday. Papal address at San Pietro (➤ 16).
New Year's Eve (31 Dec): fireworks, free concerts and massive *cenone* (dinners) in many restaurants.

Practical Matters

Above: *shopping in San Marco, Venice*
Right: *a sharp-dressed man from Milan*

TIME DIFFERENCES

GMT	Italy	Germany	USA (NY)	Netherlands	Spain
12 noon	1PM	1PM	7AM	1PM	1PM

BEFORE YOU GO

WHAT YOU NEED

● Required
○ Suggested
▲ Not required

Some countries require a pasport to remain valid for a minimum period (usually at least six months) beyond the date of entry – contact their consulate or embassy or your travel agent for details.

	UK	Germany	USA	Netherlands	Spain
Passport/National Identity Card	●	●	●	●	●
Visa	▲	▲	▲	▲	▲
Return Ticket	▲	▲	▲	▲	▲
Health Inoculations	▲	▲	▲	▲	▲
Health Documentation (reciprocal agreement document, ➤ 123)	●	●	▲	●	●
Travel Insurance	○	○	○	○	○
Driving Licence (National)	●	●	●	●	●
Car Insurance Certificate	○	○	○	○	○
Car Registration Document	●	●	●	●	●

WHEN TO GO

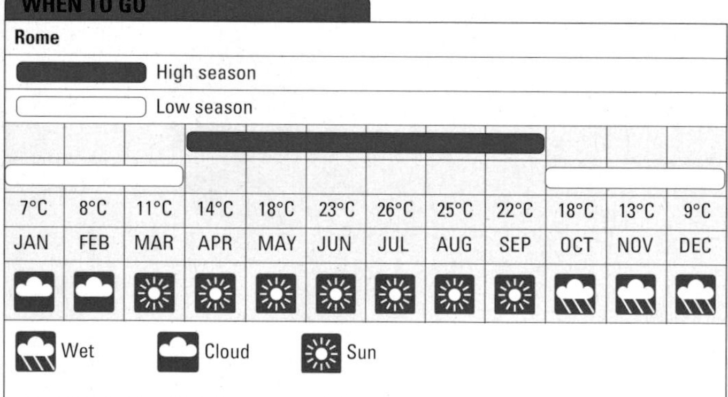

Rome

High season
Low season

JAN	FEB	MAR	APR	MAY	JUN	JUL	AUG	SEP	OCT	NOV	DEC
Low	Low	Low	High	High	High	High	High	High	Low	Low	Low
7°C	8°C	11°C	14°C	18°C	23°C	26°C	25°C	22°C	18°C	13°C	9°C
Cloud	Cloud	Sun	Sun	Sun	Sun	Sun	Sun	Sun	Wet	Wet	Wet

Wet   Cloud   Sun

TOURIST OFFICES

In the UK
Italian State Tourist Board
1 Princes Street
London W1R 8AY
☎ 020 7408 1254
Fax: 020 7493 6695

In the USA
Italian State Tourist Board
630 Fifth Avenue
Suite 1565
New York NY 10111
☎ (212) 245-4822
Fax: (212) 586-9249

Italian State Tourist Board
12400 Wilshire Boulevard
Suite 550
Los Angeles, CA 90025
☎ (310) 820-1959
Fax: (310) 820-6357

POLICE 113 *CARABINIERI* 112

FIRE 115

ANY EMERGENCY (including AMBULANCE) 118

ROAD ASSISTANCE (ACI) 116

WHEN YOU ARE THERE

ARRIVING

There are direct flights from Europe and North America to Italy's major international airports. Rome's main airport is Leonardo da Vinci, also known as Fiumicino ☎ 06 65 951. Milan has two airports, Internazionale Forlanini ☎ 02 7485 2200 and Intercontinentale della Malpensa (☎ 02 5858 3002).

Leonardo da Vinci (Fiumicino) Airport, Rome
Distance to city centre

26 kilometres

Journey times

Train	30 or 45 minutes
Bus	50 minutes
Car	40 minutes

Forlanini Airport, Milan
Distance to city centre

7 kilometres

Journey times

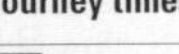

Train	N/A
Bus	30–40 minutes
Car	15 minutes

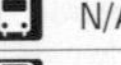

MONEY

Since 1 January 2002, the lira has given way to the Euro, which is divided into 100 cents (or *centesimi)*. Coins come in denominations of 1, 2, 5, 10, 20 and 50 cents, 1 and 2 Euros, and notes come in 5, 10, 20, 50, 100, 200 and 500 Euro denominations (the last two are rarely seen). The notes and one side of the coins are the same throughout the European single currency zone, but each country has a different design on one face of each of the coins. Notes and coins from any of the other countries can be used in Italy.

TIME

Italy is one hour ahead of Greenwich Mean Time (GMT+1), but from late March, when clocks are put forward one hour, to late October, Italian Summer Time (GMT+2) operates.

CUSTOMS

YES

From another EU country for personal use (guidelines)
800 cigarettes, 200 cigars,
1 kilogram of tobacco
10 litres of spirits (over 22%)
20 litres of aperitifs
90 litres of wine, of which 60 litres can be sparkling wine
110 litres of beer

From a non-EU country for your personal use, the allowances are:
200 cigarettes OR
50 cigars OR
250 grams of tobacco
1 litre of spirits (over 22%)
2 litres of intermediary products (eg sherry) and sparkling wine
2 litres of still wine
50 grammes of perfume
0.25 litres of eau de toilette
The value limit for goods is €175

Travellers under 17 years of age are not entitled to the tobacco and alcohol allowances.

NO

Unlicensed drugs, firearms, ammunition, offensive weapons, obscene material, unlicensed animals, counterfeit and copied goods.

EMBASSIES AND CONSULATES

UK
06 482 5441

Germany
06 492 131

USA
06 46 741

Netherlands
06 332 1141

Spain
06 684 0401

WHEN YOU ARE THERE

TOURIST OFFICES

- Florence
  Via Manzoni 16
  ☎ 055 23 320;
  www.firenze.turismo.toscana.it

- Genoa
  Palazzina Santa Maria,
  Area Porto Antico
  ☎ 01 24 871;
  www.apt.genova.it

- Milan
  Palazzo del Turismo
  Via Marconi 1
  ☎ 02 725 241

- Comune di Milano information office
  Galleria Vittorio Emanuele II
  ☎ 02 869 0734;
  www.inlombardia.it

- Naples
  Piazza dei Martiri 58
  ☎ 081 405 311

- Palermo
  Piazza Castelnuovo 34/35
  ☎ 091 583 847

- Rome
  Via Parigi 5
  ☎ 06 4889 9253
  There are information kiosks near many of the main tourist sights.

- Venice
  San Marco 717c
  ☎ 041 520 8964;
  www.provincia.venezia.it.aptv

Virtually any town or village you visit will have its own small tourist office or *Pro Loco* with maps and information leaflets.

NATIONAL HOLIDAYS

J	F	M	A	M	J	J	A	S	O	N	D
2		1	2	1			1			1	3

1 Jan	New Year's Day
6 Jan	Epiphany
Mar/Apr	Easter Monday
25 Apr	Liberation Day, 1945
1 May	Labour Day
15 Aug	Assumption of the Virgin
1 Nov	All Saints' Day
8 Dec	Immaculate Conception
25 Dec	Christmas Day
26 Dec	St Stephen's Day

Banks, businesses and most shops and museums close on these days. Most cities, towns and villages celebrate their patron saint's day, but generally, most places remain open.

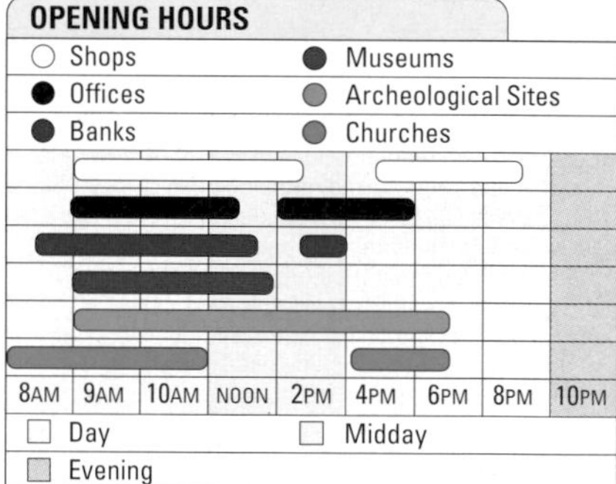

Department stores, some supermarkets, and shops in tourist areas may not close at lunchtime, and sometimes remain open until later in the evening. Some shops shut on Monday morning and may close on Saturday afternoon in summer. Most shops close on Sunday. Some banks are open until 2PM and do not reopen in the afternoon. Many museums now open in the afternoon (usually 5–7:30PM), others are open all day, and a few open late into the evening. Many museums close early on Sunday (around 1PM) and most are closed Monday.

PUBLIC TRANSPORT

Internal Flights Services throughout the country are provided by Alitalia (☎ 06 65 643). A more limited list of destinations is offered by Meridiana (☎ 02 584 171) and Air One (☎ 848 848 880 (freephone)).

Trains Italian State Railways (Ferrovie dello Stato, or FS; www.fs-on-line.com) provide an efficient (if slightly confusing) range of services. *Regionale*, *Diretto* and *Espresso* trains stop at every station and are slow for long journeys; *Intercity* trains cost more but are faster; and the *Pendolino* is the fastest and most expensive service.

Long Distance Buses There is no national bus company but Eurolines (☎ 055 357 110) offers a service between the main Italian towns and several cities outside Italy. Each major city has its own companies for short-, medium- and some long-distance coach travel.

Ferries Genoa and Naples are the main ports for the Mediterranean, with regular services to Sicily and Sardinia. Naples also has services to Capri and other islands. On the Adriatic, Brindisi and Otranto are well served by ferries to Greece. Book well in advance for car ferries.

Urban Transport Buses are the best way to get around towns of any size. Bus stops (*fermata*) are clearly marked with the routes. You need a ticket before boarding at the rear (*salita*) where you stamp it in the machine. Exit through the middle door (*uscita*). Some cities have trams, which run like buses. Venice has water buses (*vaporetti*), and Milan and Rome have underground trains. Tickets for urban public transport can be bought in tobacconists and news-stands.

CAR RENTAL

Car rental (*autonoleggio*) is available at airports, main railway stations and town-centre offices. It is relatively cheap. Small local firms offer the best rates but cars can only be booked locally. Air and train travellers can book inclusive deals.

TAXIS

Taxis can be hailed in the street, found at taxi ranks (stations and major *piazze*), or phoned. There's an initial charge and a rate per kilometre. Heavy traffic can mean stiff meter increases and there are Sunday and late-night supplements.

DRIVING

Speed limit on motorways (*autostrade*), which have tolls: **130kph**

Speed limit on main roads: **110kph**; secondary roads: **90kph**

Speed limit on urban roads: **50kph**

Seat belts must be worn in front seats at all times and in rear seats where fitted.

Random breath-testing is frequent. Alcohol limit: 80mg per 100ml blood.

Petrol (*benzina*) is expensive. All garages sell unleaded (*senza piombo*). Outside urban areas filling stations open 7–12:30 and 3–7:30. Motorway services open 24 hours. Credit cards aren't widely accepted away from these. Some automatic pumps take banknotes.

In the event of a breakdown, ☎ 116, giving your registration number and type of car, and the nearest ACI (Automobile Club d'Italia) office will assist you. This service is free to foreign-registered vehicles or cars rented from Rome or Milan airports (you will need to present your passport).

PERSONAL SAFETY

Particularly in busy towns and tourist spots, petty theft is the main problem. The *carabinieri*, to whom thefts should be reported, wear black uniforms with red stripes down the outer seams of the trousers. Some precautions:
Carry shoulder bags and cameras slung across your body. Scooter-borne bag-snatchers can be foiled if you keep on the inside of the pavement. Do not put anything down on a café or restaurant table. Lock car doors and never keep valuables in your car.

***Carabinieri* assistance:**
☎ 112 from any call box

TELEPHONES

Almost every bar in Italy has a telephone, and there are many in public places. Most of them operate with phonecards (*schede telefoniche*) for €2.5, €5 or €16, which can be bought from tobacconists, bars, post offices, news-stands and other public places. Some take coins of 10, 20 or 50 cents, €1 or €2 and some take credit cards.

International Dialling Codes	
From Italy to:	
UK:	**00 44**
Germany:	**00 49**
USA/Canada:	**00 1**
Netherlands:	**00 31**

POST

Post Offices
Rome's main post office is on Piazza San Silvestro.
🕓 Mon–Fri 9–6, Sat 9–2, Sun 9–8
☎ 160

Other post offices
🕓 Mon–Fri 8–1:30 or 2, Sat 8–1 (these times may vary slightly). Closed Sun.

ELECTRICITY

The power supply is 220 volts (125 volts in parts of Italy). Type of socket: round two- or three-hole sockets taking plugs of two round pins, or sometimes three pins in a vertical line. British visitors should bring an adaptor, US visitors will need a voltage transformer.

TIPS/GRATUITIES

Yes ✓ No ✗		
Hotels (service not inc)	✓	10–15%
Restaurants (service not inc)	✓	10–15%
Cafés/bars	✓	100 cents min
Taxis	✓	15%
Porters	✓	1
Chambermaids	✓	2 weekly
Hairdressers	✓	2
Cloakroom attendants	✓	1
Toilets	✓	100 cents min

In general the light in Italy is good, although on sunny days there can be a bit of glare (particularly in the south) and in the north the light can be hazy.
Where you can photograph: Most museums and certain churches will not allow you to photograph inside; check first.
Film and developing: A roll of film is called a *pellicola*, but 'film' should get you understood. Film and developing are more expensive in Italy than in the UK or USA.

HEALTH

Insurance

Nationals of EU and certain other countries receive reduced cost medical (including hospital) treatment and pay a percentage for prescribed medicines. You need a qualifying document (Form E111 for Britons). Private medical insurance is still advised.

Dental Services

Nationals of EU and certain other countries can obtain dental treatment at a reduced cost from dentists within the Italian health service. A qualifying document (Form 111 for Britons) is needed. Private medical insurance is still advised.

Sun Advice

In summer, particularly in July and August, it can get oppressively hot and humid in cities. If 'doing the sights', cover up and apply a sunscreen (or dive into the shade of a museum), and take in plenty of fluids.

Drugs

A pharmacy (*farmacia*), recognised by a green cross sign, will possess highly trained staff able to offer medical advice on minor ailments and provide a wide range of prescribed and non-prescribed medicines and drugs.

Safe Water

In some isolated rural areas it is not advisable to drink the tap water. However, across most of the rest of the country the water is perfectly safe, although most Italians prefer to drink bottled mineral water.

CONCESSIONS

Students/Youths Holders of an International Student Identity Card (ISIC) and, for those under 26, an International Youth Card (IYC) can take advantage of discounts on transport, accommodation, museum entrance fees, car rental and in restaurants. Nationals (under 18) of EU and certain other countries receive free admission to state museums.
Senior Citizens Citizens aged over 60 of EU and other countries with which Italy has a reciprocal arrangement (not including the USA) may gain free admission to some museums and receive discounts at others and on public transport on production of their passport.

CLOTHING SIZES

Italy	UK	Europe	USA	
46	36	46	36	Suits
48	38	48	38	
50	40	50	40	
52	42	52	42	
54	44	54	44	
56	46	56	46	
41	7	41	8	Shoes
42	7.5	42	8.5	
43	8.5	43	9.5	
44	9.5	44	10.5	
45	10.5	45	11.5	
46	11	46	12	
37	14.5	37	14.5	Shirts
38	15	38	15	
39/40	15.5	39/40	15.5	
41	16	41	16	
42	16.5	42	16.5	
43	17	43	17	
36	8	34	6	Dresses
38	10	36	8	
40	12	38	10	
42	14	40	12	
44	16	42	14	
46	18	44	16	
38	4.5	38	6	Shoes
38	5	38	6.5	
39	5.5	39	7	
39	6	39	7.5	
40	6.5	40	8	
41	7	41	8.5	

- Contact the airport or airline on the day prior to leaving to ensure the flight details are unchanged.
- The airport departure tax, payable when you leave Italy, is included in the cost of your airline ticket.
- Check the duty-free limits of the country you are travelling to before departure.

LANGUAGE

Italian is the native language, but each region has its own dialect, with its own particular stresses and vocabulary, which can be difficult to understand. Many Italians, especially in tourist areas, speak a little English, but you will be better received if you at least attempt to communicate in Italian. Italian words are pronounced phonetically. Every vowel and consonant (except 'h') is sounded. Below are a few words that may be helpful. More extensive coverage can be found in the AA's *Essential Italian Phrase Book* which lists over 2,000 phrases and 2,000 words.

hotel	*albergo*	rate	*tariffa*
room	*camera*	breakfast	*prima colazione*
...single/double	*...singola/doppia*	toilet	*bagno/toilette*
for one/two nights	*per una/due notte/i*	bathroom	*bagno*
		shower	*doccia*
for one/two people	*per una/due persona/e*	balcony	*balcone*
		key	*chiave*
reservation	*prenotazione*	chambermaid	*cameriera*

bank	*banco*	coin	*moneta*
exchange office	*ufficio di cambio*	credit card	*carta di credito*
post office	*posta*	travellers' cheque	*assegno turistico*
cashier	*cassiere/a*	exchange rate	*tasso di cambio*
automatic cash dispenser	*sportello automatico*	commission charge	*commissione*
foreign currency	*valuta estera*	change	*resto*
bank note	*banconota*	pound sterling	*sterlina*

restaurant	*ristorante*	main course	*il secondo*
café/bar	*bar*	dish of the day	*piatto del giorno*
table	*tavolo*	dessert	*dolce*
menu	*lista/carta/menu*	drink	*bevanda*
wine list	*lista dei vini*	waiter	*cameriere*
lunch	*pranzo*	waitress	*cameriera*
dinner	*cena*	the bill	*il conto*
starter	*il primo*	beer	*birra*

airport	*aeroporto*	..single/return	*andata sola/ andata e ritorno*
train	*treno*		
..station	*stazione ferroviaria*	ticket office	*biglietteria*
		timetable	*orario*
bus	*autobus*	seat	*posto*
..station	*autostazione*	non-smoking	*vietato fumare*
ferry	*traghetto*	reserved	*prenotato/ riservato*
ticket	*biglietto*		

yes	*si*	where?	*dove?*
no	*no*	today	*oggi*
please	*per favore*	tomorrow	*domani*
thank you	*grazie*	yesterday	*ieri*
hello	*salve*	how much?	*quanto costa?*
goodbye	*arrivederci/ ciao!*	expensive	*caro*
		open	*aperto*
excuse me	*mi scusi*	closed	*chiuso*
sorry	*mi dispiace*	you're welcome	*di niente/nulla*
help!	*aiuto*	that's all right	*prego*

INDEX

Acknowledgements
The Automobile Association wishes to thank the following photographers and libraries for their assistance in the preparation of this book:

STEVE DAY 47; JOHN HESELTINE ARCHIVE 49, 84b; HULTON GETTY 11b, 11c; MARY EVANS PICTURE LIBRARY 10b, 14b, 14c; SPECTRUM COLOUR LIBRARY 34, 37; WORLD PICTURES 48, 83b, www.euro.ecb.int 119 (euro notes).

The remaining photographs are held in the Association's own library (AA PHOTO LIBRARY) and were taken by Clive Sawyer, with the exception of pages 15b, 35b taken by Pete Bennett; 60c taken by Peter Davies; F/cover (a) plaque, Florence, 54, 66 taken by Jerry Edmanson; 9c, 16, 17a, 17b, 27b, 71, 72, 73, 77a, 77b, 79, 122c taken by Jim Holmes; F/cover (d) scooter, Naples taken by Max Jourdan; 12c taken by Julian Loader; 68c taken by Eric Meacher; 8b, 15a, 16a, 18a, 19a, 20a, 22a, 23a, 24a, 25a, 26a, 39a, 44b, 45b, 74, 117a taken by Dario Mitidieri; F/cover (e) Duomo, Florence, (g) sunflower, Tuscany, 6b, 7c, 52, 55, 57, 60b, 63,65, 67, 68b, 91a, 92-116 taken by Ken Paterson; 21b, 122b taken by Barrie Smith; 5a. 5B, 6a, 7a, 8a, 9a, 9b, 10a, 11a, 12a, 14a, 25b, 27a, 28a, 29, 30, 33, 35a, 36a, 38a, 64, 69a, 86b, 88b taken by Antony Souter; F/cover bottom pasta taken by Wyn Voysey; F/cover (h) sculpture, Rome, (i) Colosseum, Rome, 76 taken by Peter Wilson

Copy editor: Audrey Horne

Dear Essential Traveller

Your comments, opinions and recommendations are very important to us. So please help us to improve our travel guides by taking a few minutes to complete this simple questionnaire.

You do not need a stamp (unless posted outside the UK). If you do not want to cut this page from your guide, then photocopy it or write your answers on a plain sheet of paper.

Send to: **The Editor, AA World Travel Guides, FREEPOST SCE 4598, Basingstoke RG21 4GY.**

Your recommendations...

We always encourage readers' recommendations for restaurants, nightlife or shopping – if your recommendation is used in the next edition of the guide, we will send you a ***FREE*** **AA *Essential* Guide** of your choice. Please state below the establishment name, location and your reasons for recommending it.

____

____

____

____

Please send me **AA *Essential*** ________________________
(*see list of titles inside the front cover*)

About this guide...

Which title did you buy?
AA *Essential* ________________________
Where did you buy it? ________________________
When? m m / y y

Why did you choose an AA *Essential* Guide? ____________________

____

____

____

____

Did this guide meet your expectations?
Exceeded ☐ Met all ☐ Met most ☐ Fell below ☐
Please give your reasons ________________________

____

____

____

continued on next page...

Were there any aspects of this guide that you particularly liked? ____________

____

____

____

Is there anything we could have done better? ____________

____

____

____

____

About you...

Name (*Mr/Mrs/Ms*) ____________________

Address ____________________

____

____________________ Postcode ____________

Daytime tel nos ____________________

Which age group are you in?

Under 25 ☐ 25–34 ☐ 35–44 ☐ 45–54 ☐ 55–64 ☐ 65+ ☐

How many trips do you make a year?

Less than one ☐ One ☐ Two ☐ Three or more ☐

Are you an AA member? Yes ☐ No ☐

About your trip...

When did you book? m m / y y When did you travel? m m / y y

How long did you stay? ____________________

Was it for business or leisure? ____________________

Did you buy any other travel guides for your trip?

If yes, which ones? ____________________

____

Thank you for taking the time to complete this questionnaire. Please send it to us as soon as possible, and remember, you do not need a stamp (*unless posted outside the UK*).

Happy Holidays!